INSIGHT FOR LIVING MINISTRIES BIBLE COMPANION
INSIGHTS AND APPLICATION FOR <u>REAL</u> LIFE

D0469604

What if…?

From the Bible-Teaching Ministry of

CHARLES R. SWINDOLL

WHAT IF . . . ?
BIBLE COMPANION

From the Bible-Teaching Ministry of Charles R. Swindoll

Charles R. Swindoll has devoted his life to the accurate, practical teaching and application of God's Word and His grace. A pastor at heart, Chuck has served as senior pastor to congregations in Texas, Massachusetts, and California. Since 1998, he has served as the founder and senior pastor-teacher of Stonebriar Community Church in Frisco, Texas, but Chuck's listening audience extends far beyond a local church body. As a leading program in Christian broadcasting since 1979, *Insight for Living* airs in major Christian radio markets around the world, reaching people groups in languages they can understand. Chuck's extensive writing ministry has also served the body of Christ worldwide and his leadership as president and now chancellor of Dallas Theological Seminary has helped prepare and equip a new generation of men and women for ministry. Chuck and Cynthia, his partner in life and ministry, have four grown children, ten grandchildren, and four great-grandchildren.

The 2014 Bible Companion text was collaboratively developed and written by John Adair and the Creative Ministries Department of Insight for Living Ministries, based upon the original outlines, charts, and transcripts of Charles R. Swindoll's sermons.

Published by:
IFL Publishing House, A Division of Insight for Living Ministries
Post Office Box 1050, Frisco, Texas 75034-0018

Editor in Chief: Cynthia Swindoll, President, Insight for Living Ministries
Executive Vice President: Wayne Stiles, Th.M., D.Min., Dallas Theological Seminary
Writer: John Adair, Th.M, Ph.D., Dallas Theological Seminary
Substantive Editor: Kathryn Robertson, M.A., English, Hardin-Simmons University
Copy Editors: Jim Craft, M.A., English, Mississippi College; Certificate of Biblical and Theological Studies, Dallas Theological Seminary
Paula McCoy, B.A., English, Texas A&M University-Commerce
Project Supervisor, Creative Ministries: Megan Meckstroth, B.S., Advertising, University of Florida
Project Coordinators, Publishing: Melissa Cleghorn, B.A., University of North Texas
Margaret Gulliford, B.A., Graphic Design, Taylor University
Proofreader: LeeAnna Swartz, B.A., Communications, Moody Bible Institute
Designer: Dameon Runnels, B.A., Art—Mass Media; B.A., Mass Communications, Grambling State University
Production Artist: Nancy Gustine, B.F.A., Advertising Art, University of North Texas

ISBN: 978-1-62655-050-6
Printed in the United States of America

Table of Contents

A Letter
from Chuck

Temptations, tests, and trials—Jesus endured them all. His short life on this planet was filled with difficulties—"a man of sorrows," as Isaiah aptly called Him (Isaiah 53:3).

When Jesus walked the highways and back roads of Israel, He experienced the wide range of sufferings and struggles that human beings have known since Adam's fall. The Bible tells us that Jesus "understands our weaknesses, for he faced all of the same testings we do, yet he did not sin" (Hebrews 4:15). We need reminders like this one, because when we walk through our own deep valleys, it's good to know that the One we follow has been there and persevered.

Keep this truth in mind as you work your way through this series, which I have called, *What If . . . ?* Each lesson in this Bible Companion presents a particular trial that most of us will grapple with at one time or another, either personally or on behalf of someone we love. Loss, relational strife, disability, and cruelty will find us all at some point and, if we haven't ever considered them, leave us confused and wondering what to do. That's why it's important to look to Scripture to prepare ourselves for the trials we haven't yet faced and to gain renewed strength to endure the ones we're living through right now.

You'll find that many of the topics covered on these pages are rarely addressed in church, yet they are present in the Bible. Jesus's perseverance and sinlessness in the face of these trials continue to speak loudly to us as we endure them today. Jesus showed us how to live in a truly human fashion—in the way we were *meant* to live.

I encourage you to pick up this volume and work through it carefully. Allow the practical advice of Scripture to season your thoughts and your actions. And as you read, remember Jesus . . . He found His way. So can you.

Charles R. Swindoll

How to Use This Bible Companion

We all have questions. We all wonder about the future. We all pose hypothetical situations and try to figure out what we might do in such and such a situation. This volume offers the opportunity to reflect on several situations to which we might not have given careful consideration. Taking the chance to think through what the Bible says about these questions will not only give us wisdom for the way ahead but will, in the process, draw us closer to the true God.

You may work through this study individually or with a group, but regardless which method you choose, a brief introduction to the overall structure of the study will help you get the most out of it.

Lesson Organization

 LET'S BEGIN HERE serves as an introduction to each lesson, highlighting the main idea for rapid orientation.

Each lesson itself is composed of two main teaching sections for insight and application:

 LET'S DIG DEEPER explores the principles of Scripture through observation and interpretation of the Bible passages, drawing out practical principles for life.

In *observation*, our goal is to see what's on the page—to gather facts. We take note of key words and phrases, names and places, comparisons and contrasts, and causes and effects.

In *interpretation*, our goal is to make sense of our observations—to determine what's spiritually significant about the facts we've gathered. We accomplish this by asking questions about history, culture, literature, and grammar. Once we've answered these questions, we reach general conclusions about the passages of Scripture under consideration.

In *correlation*, parallel passages and additional questions supplement the main Scripture passages for a more in-depth study.

 LET'S LIVE IT focuses on application, helping you put into practice the principles of each lesson in ways that fit your personality, gifts, and level of spiritual maturity.

Using the Bible Companion

The *What If . . . ? Bible Companion* is designed for individuals, but it may be adapted for group study. If you choose to use this Bible Companion in a group setting, please keep in mind that many of the lessons ask personal, probing questions, seeking to reveal true character and challenge the reader to change. Some answers may be embarrassing if shared in a group setting. Care, therefore, should be taken by the leader to prepare the group for the sensitive nature of the study, to forego certain questions that appear too personal, and to remain perceptive to the mood and dynamics of the group, redirecting as questions or answers become uncomfortable.

Whether you use this Bible Companion in a group or individually, we recommend the following method:

Prayer — Begin each lesson with prayer, asking God to teach you through His Word and to open your heart to the self-discovery afforded by the questions and text of the lesson.

Scripture — Have your Bible handy. We recommend the New American Standard Bible, The New Living Translation, or another literal translation, rather than a paraphrase. As you progress through each lesson, you'll be prompted to read relevant sections of Scripture and answer questions related to the topic. You'll also want to look up the Scripture passages noted in parentheses.

Questions—As you encounter the questions, approach them wisely and creatively. Not every question will be applicable to every person every time. Use the questions as general guidelines for your thinking rather than rigid forms to complete. If there are things you just don't understand or want to explore further, be sure to jot down your thoughts and questions.

Special Bible Companion Features

Throughout the chapters, you'll find several special features designed to add insight and depth to your study. Use these features to enhance your study and to deepen your knowledge of Scripture, history, and theology.

 GETTING TO THE ROOT
While our English versions of Scripture are reliable, studying the original languages can often bring to light nuances of the text that are sometimes missed in translation. This feature explores the underlying meanings of the words or phrases in particular passages, sometimes providing parallel examples to illuminate the meaning of the inspired biblical text.

 A CLOSER LOOK
Various passages in Scripture touch on deeper theological or prophetic questions. This feature will help you gain deeper insight into specific theological issues related to the biblical text.

 DOORWAY TO HISTORY
Sometimes the chronological gap that separates us from the original author and the original readers clouds our understanding of Scripture. This feature takes you back in time to explore the surrounding history, culture, and customs of the ancient world.

Our prayer is that this Insight for Living Ministries Bible Companion will not only help you dig deeper into God's Word but also provide insights and application for *real* life.

What if...?

What If God Chooses You to Do Something Great?

EXODUS 3:1–8, 10–11, 13–15; 4:1–4, 10–11, 13, 29–31

LET'S BEGIN HERE

Our Lord is full of surprises! His leading includes twists and turns, ups and downs, potholes and drop-offs that initially shake us up. The fact that we rarely can guess the ultimate destination only adds to the adventure! God's plans for us are often over and above what we imagine or desire . . . and our response is often reluctance. Yet God continues to stretch us beyond what we consider our limits. The Bible includes numerous examples of individuals whom God used to accomplish great things, but rather than immediately embracing the challenge and trusting His enablement, they held back. They were unwilling to leave the shallow waters of the familiar to dive into the depths of His audacious plan, because they feared the unknown. In this lesson we'll meet a man who felt that way—an obscure, 80-year-old shepherd whose failure broke his spirit and left him feeling "over the hill" and washed up. Little did he know—he was on the verge of something great.

LET'S DIG DEEPER

Montgomery, Alabama, in the 1950s was a divided city. Segregation on buses and in other community areas throughout the city made concrete the racial divide that had originated in the area's early history, pre- and post-Civil War. The region's strong ties to Christianity and the faith's hope in a kingdom composed of all nations underlined the bitter irony of the unjust system. Surely many wondered, *What impact can one person have in the face of such systemic injustice?*

It turns out . . . plenty.

In 1955, a middle-aged seamstress named Rosa Parks quietly refused to give up her seat at the front of a segregated bus. When Parks landed in jail for disobeying the order of the bus driver, the new pastor of a moderately sized church in Montgomery spearheaded a boycott of the city's segregated bus system. That reverend's name? Martin Luther King, Jr.

Many self-identified Christians in Montgomery had long gone along in silence with the unjust treatment of their fellow citizens. It took two bold voices to put change in motion. By standing up for those who were mistreated and oppressed by the powerful and the privileged, Parks, King, and eventually many others, gained a measure of greatness. King ultimately stood before more than a quarter of a million people in the power-center of the United States and painted a picture of his dream—one that made numerous, explicit biblical references to the prophetic vision of God's kingdom.

Around the world and throughout human history, God has called many to greatness. These men and women have stood against evil, helped those in need, and cared for the things God cares for. Yet among this group, many have come from humble beginnings.

Name someone from humble beginnings whom God used to accomplish great things. Then explain what came about through this person's obedience.

Why do you think so many people presume that God won't do something great in their lives?

_____

_____

_____

_____

In Our Brokenness: Three Frequent Mistakes

Certainly, God can do a great work through *anyone*. Centuries before Rosa Parks and Martin Luther King, Jr., God called another person—an older, isolated shepherd—to stand up for the oppressed. God's choice seemed a surprise, most especially to the shepherd, Moses.

Moses's response to such a great calling wasn't unique. He demonstrated three mistakes believers often make when we finally accept the prospect of God's good work in *us*.

First, *because of intensity, we run before we're sent*. When we buy into the idea that God could actually do something great through us, we throw ourselves into life with a new intensity. Unfortunately, that often means we step out before the Lord says "Go!" When Moses began to understand his calling, he killed an oppressive Egyptian—on impulse, not on God's command (Exodus 2:11–12). Moses ran before God sent him.

Read Exodus 2:11–12. What do you think motivated Moses to act the way he did in this passage?

_____

_____

_____

_____

Read 1 Samuel 24:1–7. What happened between David and Saul in this passage, and what conviction motivated David to act the way he did?

_____

_____

_____

_____

Contrast David's actions with those of Moses. Given what you know about God's plan to rescue His people, what do you believe Moses should have done differently?

_____

_____

_____

_____

_____

Second, _because of insecurity, we retreat after we've failed._ When we attempt something great on God's behalf but it doesn't work out, our insecurities rise. And invariably, insecurity leads us to retreat from the great work before us. Moses, who desired to help his enslaved people, ran ahead of God, killed a man, and then fled into the desert. Moses's insecurity led him to retreat after he had failed.

The third mistake we make happens as a result of our misunderstanding how God works: _because of inferiority, we resist when we're called._ We often believe our limitations mean that God cannot work through us. Therefore, we resist His call, naively believing that God's great work depends on our ability rather than His. Moses again proves to be a worthy example here, as he gave the Lord excuse after excuse why he couldn't go before Pharaoh.

When God Speaks: Four Common Answers

God has used many people for His glory, but in Scripture, Moses's life is particularly compelling due to his humble origins and his significant role in Israel's history. Let's take a closer look at his story.

 Read Exodus 3:1–12.

Though Moses lived in Pharaoh's palace as a young man, he spent his middle years in the desert of Midian, nowhere near the power-center of Egypt. More importantly, the desert life isolated Moses from God's people. Yet, his estrangement didn't remove the shepherd from God's sight.

One day, after forty years in the desert, Moses received a miraculous visit from the Lord. As the shepherd led his flocks to graze in the desert, he happened upon a bush aflame. The sight wouldn't have been completely out of the ordinary; the intense desert heat sometimes reacted with the sap of bushes and created flames. The miracle was that the bush burned *without being consumed*. This continual burning got the shepherd's attention, and from within the bush, the Lord spoke (Exodus 3:2–3).

 DOORWAY TO HISTORY
Was Jesus at the Burning Bush?
Early Christians read the Bible with Jesus on their minds. So when they turned to the Old Testament, they wondered what in that collection of ancient texts pointed forward to the Son. Many early Christians saw the Son in those Old Testament accounts in which the Lord appeared to a human being. So when second-century theologians like Justin Martyr read the account of the burning bush, they saw Jesus there speaking to Moses.

Continued on next page

Continued from previous page

The reasoning behind this thinking was simple, and it came from Jesus Himself: no one has seen the Father except for Jesus Himself (John 6:46). Therefore, when the Lord appeared in the Old Testament, it had to be Jesus, rather than the Father.

Why is knowing the specific identity of the voice in the bush important? Because it reveals the multi-personal nature of God *before* Jesus took on human flesh. Further, it creates a tension in the way that we think about God. Yes, He has come near in Christ, but according to John 6:46, we understand that the Father remains unseen by us. God the Father stands removed from humanity, accessible only through His Son, Jesus Christ. In this way, we encounter the true expansiveness of God, who is far beyond our understanding. The presence of the Son at the burning bush reminds us that God is both near and far from us. He simply cannot be contained by our experiences or thoughts. The Father's greatness reminds us of our humble state, which prompts us to trust Him.

As the Lord announced His presence to Moses, the shepherd showed a standard response: he "covered his face because he was afraid" (Exodus 3:6). Like other biblical figures who encountered the Almighty, Moses was immediately aware of his humble position. The Lord then informed the shepherd of His plans: God wanted His people set free from their Egyptian slavery . . . and He wanted Moses to speak to Pharaoh for Him.

God called Moses to a great work, but Moses could think of nothing but resisting the call. He didn't believe he was significant enough to do the job. Of course, Moses was absolutely right! If God's people were going to be set free, God Himself would have to do it. However, God promised His presence to Moses, assuring him that he was the Lord's choice. Yet, the 80-year-old shepherd continued to focus on himself and made excuses to avoid going back to Pharaoh's palace.

Read Exodus 3:13–4:17.

First, Moses told God, *"I will not have all the answers."* Faced with the prospect of standing before his own people again, Moses pictured himself struggling to find the words to respond to questions that might arise. The old, desert-dwelling shepherd didn't feel confident about speaking for God or identifying Him before strangers. What if the Hebrews asked Moses about the identity of this God? What would Moses say? The thought terrified him, even though God gave Moses the answers that should've calmed his mind. The Lord told Moses to tell the Hebrews that "I AM" sent him. In other words, Moses was to go to the people, believing that the God who exists was behind him. This should have brought confidence to the old man . . . but it didn't.

Can you think of another biblical figure who didn't have all the answers? How did God work in that individual's life?

_____

_____

_____

_____

Consider Job's suffering and eventual encounter with the Lord. Job wanted to know why such a mountain of suffering had come upon him even though he was righteous. Did Job get his questions answered? (See Job 38 – 42.)

_____

_____

_____

_____

What does Job's encounter with God tell us about having all the answers?

_____

_____

_____

_____

Moses offered a second excuse: *"I may not have all their respect."* Moses worried that the people wouldn't believe that God had actually appeared to him. Why should they believe the message of a killer who had fled from justice decades earlier? God again patiently answered Moses's concerns, demonstrating His miraculous power in order to soothe the shepherd's doubts.

However, God's demonstration still wasn't enough for Moses, who then told the Lord, *"I don't have all the ability."* Moses was caught up with thinking about what *he* could do, rather than what God could do through him. So Moses pointed out the limitations of his own speech, a physical problem he couldn't overcome. But Moses was talking to the One who created his mouth! If anyone could work through a human mouth — even a damaged one — it was the Creator Himself.

Moses tried one more excuse: *"I am not as qualified as others."* In other words, Moses directly asked the Lord to send someone else (Exodus 4:13). While the first three excuses could've been construed as legitimate concerns, Moses's fourth objection displayed a stubborn unwillingness to obey. This fired the anger of God, who abruptly appointed Aaron to lead the people out of Egypt alongside Moses.

When God puts us in a position to accomplish a particular task, He wants us to follow through. Read Matthew 26:36 – 44. How did Jesus respond to the task before Him on the eve of His crucifixion?

_____

_____

_____

_____

 LET'S LIVE IT

As we examine the exchange between God and Moses at the burning bush, two essential perspectives emerge. We would do well to consider them carefully.

First, *never, ever believe that God is through doing great things.* God did great things again and again in Scripture. If He could do it then, He can do it now. Indeed, our continued faith in the Lord means that we believe He continues to do great things. We know this includes saving people. And we know that one day, He will resurrect all of humanity either to life or to judgment.

Take a few minutes to recall some of the great things of God that you've witnessed. List them below.

_____

_____

_____

_____

What responses does your list create in you?

_____

_____

_____

_____

Second, *never, ever think that God is through doing great things through you.* When we look at Moses, we see a deeply flawed man who took matters into his own hands by killing an Egyptian and then, after forty years in the desert, resisting God's plan for delivering His people. God has always done great things through flawed people! He can, therefore, do great things through you.

While it's impossible to know if a great thing is on your horizon, you can prepare yourself to respond well when God reveals that He wants to use you. On the lines below, write a prayer committing yourself to God's desire for your life.

_____

_____

_____

_____

_____

God's gracious deliverance of the Hebrews from their Egyptian slavery required a great work, and God chose Moses for that work. But Moses has long since died, and the Lord's work in the world isn't finished. Today, He chooses other flawed people to do great things. Don't shy away from whatever it is God wants to accomplish through your life. Commit your entire self to Him . . . and something great just might happen.

LESSON TWO

What If You Suddenly Lose Everything?

JOB 1:1–3, 6–11, 20–21; 2:1–6, 8–10; JAMES 4:13–16

LET'S BEGIN HERE

All of us would agree—life is difficult. Without warning, heartbreaking moments and tragic events cut our legs out from under us and drop us on our faces. Caught by surprise, we wonder if our anguish is truly unbearable. It's bad enough when such pain comes as the result of our wrongdoing—when we suffer the awful consequences of our own disobedience. However, little compares to the pain we're called upon to endure when we don't deserve it. Picture someone who walks in integrity, loves God, and treats others with kindness and grace and mercy . . . and then, suddenly, loses everything. How could this happen? And could it happen to you? Who knows? The experience may be just around the corner.

Are you ready?

LET'S DIG DEEPER

In the early morning hours of August 29, 2005, a powerful, category 3 hurricane made landfall just east of New Orleans, Louisiana. Despite evacuation efforts, approximately 100,000 people remained in the city as the hurricane dropped more than 8 inches of rain. More significantly, the storm surge swelled to twenty feet near New Orleans, and when the poorly designed levees broke, ten feet of water covered more than 80 percent of the city. In the aftermath, almost 2,000 people in Louisiana, Mississippi, and three other states were dead, while the population of New Orleans was cut in half due to unlivable conditions in hundreds of thousands of homes.[1]

Talk about losing everything! The people of this hard-hit region suffered loss of all kinds. The death toll was unprecedented in modern American storms. Material devastation led to broken, rotting homes that forced people to leave the only city they had ever called home. And even after the water receded, emotional scars lingered.

Though we will never be free of mysterious, tragic events like Hurricane Katrina, we often live as if such things won't touch us. Worse, many of us take on a smug air, believing we *deserve* a cushy existence. And then, when the reality of sin breaks into our lives, we're left to struggle over the ash heap, ill-prepared to deal with suffering in an appropriate, God-honoring fashion.

Have you ever "lost everything?" If so, describe your experience. If not, describe a situation when you were significantly touched by the brokenness of our world.

_____

_____

_____

_____

_____

What was your response in the wake of that tragedy? How have you coped since?

_____

_____

_____

_____

_____

Let's Learn about Job's Tragic Losses

The struggle with loss stretches back across the wide expanse of human history. In those ancient times lived a man who lost everything. His name was Job.

 Read Job 1:1–19; 2:1–9.

To give the tragedies in Job's life context, Scripture begins its portrait of Job by painting him as a blameless, upright person (Job 1:1). This doesn't mean Job was perfect, but simply that he didn't traffic sin into his life. Furthermore, the introduction of Job as a good man reminds us up front that suffering comes to all people. Goodness didn't exempt Job from suffering; neither does it exempt us.

What was the extent of Job's tragedy? First, Satan caused Job to lose all his livestock, his many servants, and his children in a single day (1:13–19). A rich man, Job had accumulated an extensive household. In the ancient world, this would've been considered a sign of blessing. Everyone, no matter their religion, saw wealth as divine blessing. That tragedy struck this virtuous, blessed man was a sign to all the book's original readers that suffering is blind. Riches and righteousness are no protection against the possibility of pain.

Job's suffering didn't stop with the loss of his possessions and family; Satan also sought to afflict Job's person. With the caveat that Satan must not kill Job, the Lord again allowed Satan to act, and the Evil One covered Job with boils (2:7). From the crown of his head to the soles of his feet, Job suffered from sores oozing pus and blood. Once again, Job's goodness didn't stop the pain. Rather, his righteousness was more the impetus for Satan.

When Job's wife, the only person left of his entire household, told him to curse God and die (2:9), Job's suffering was just about complete. Satan had removed all possibility of comfort that Job might find in his immediate household. By the end of chapter 2, the poor man was alone, with only physical, emotional, and marital suffering to keep him company.

What regular practice did Job have before his suffering began, according to Job 1:5?

_____

_____

_____

_____

What does this tell you about Job's faith in relation to his family?

_____

_____

_____

_____

We don't make burnt offerings, but we do offer prayers for those we love. What does the portrayal of Job as a regular intercessor for his children and their eventual death suggest about the nature of suffering?

_____

_____

_____

_____

What kinds of prayers do you think you could continually offer for others, knowing that there is nothing you can do to stop your loved ones from suffering?

_____

_____

_____

_____

A CLOSER LOOK
Satan Around Every Corner?

Lots of Christians look for Satan behind every bush. Wake up in a sour mood? Must be Satan. Argue with a family member? Satan strikes again. Bad weather wreaks havoc on the commute? Who else could be working in that? No one but Satan!

Those who see Satan in all of life's negatives often point to Job 2 as evidence: the Lord used Satan to test Job; therefore, all the negatives that happen in our lives are also the work of Satan. However, that conclusion doesn't follow the evidence. Satan certainly did afflict Job, but there's nothing in the Bible to suggest that all suffering is a result of similar testing. Satan brought about Job's suffering, but that doesn't mean we should see the Devil behind every negative in our own lives. There are at least four causes of our suffering.

- Satan: Job 1–2 is the classic passage explicating Satan's role in human suffering, as he pled with God for the opportunity to bring pain to Job. But Satan's rare appearances in Scripture give way to other, more significant causes of human suffering . . .

- Personal Sin: Much of what befalls us we bring upon ourselves through our own sin or weakness. King Saul lived much of his reign in anguish after his disobedience left him outside of God's plans for the future (1 Samuel 15:24–28).

- The Sins of Others: We often suffer the consequences of someone else's sin. Daniel was exiled to Babylon not because of something he did but because the sins of his forefathers led God to decide that exile was in order.

Continued on next page

Continued from previous page

- A Broken World: Finally, many things happen in this world as a result of the brokenness that comes with the presence of sin. All is not as it should be. Hurricanes wreak destruction. Fires decimate homes. Sin has broken our world.

So where does *your* suffering come from? The Bible offers no evidence that Job ever knew about Satan's role in his ill health or the death of his children, servants, and livestock. Suggesting as much in our own lives is probably taking it a step too far. Rather, our suffering should prompt us to correct wickedness in our own lives, forgive those who have sinned against us, and reach out to God for comfort and guidance as we seek to persevere in the righteousness to which He has called us.

Let's Observe How Job Responded

The first two chapters in the book of Job don't merely recount the man's suffering. They also show us the two responses he had to his pain.

Read Job 1:20–21; 2:10.

First, Job grieved the loss of his children, servants, and livestock. Tearing one's robe and shaving one's head were traditional ways of expressing grief in the ancient world. These acts would've indicated the deep sorrow in a person's heart. Notice that in the midst of Job's grief, he also fell to the ground and worshiped (Job 1:20). Grief and worship are not mutually exclusive. One need not stop grieving before one can worship. In fact, Job's grief spurred him to worship.

Consider Job's words in Job 1:21. Describe the significance of his statement about birth and death in light of the fact that he had just lost his children, servants, and livestock.

_____

_____

_____

_____

What does "The LORD gave me what I had, /and the LORD has taken it away. / Praise the name of the LORD!" reveal about Job's perspective in the midst of his grief?

_____

_____

_____

_____

Given Job's example, how do you think faith should function in the midst of grief?

_____

_____

_____

_____

Job believed that God was sovereign, that the Lord would give and take as He saw fit. After losing his health, that belief was put to the test as Job's distraught wife offered him this advice: "Curse God and die!" (Job 2:9). Then came Job's second response to his pain: he remained constant in his faith.

Job discerned the situation properly and remained rooted in what he knew about the Lord. Therefore, Job responded by likening his wife's words to those of foolish women. But he didn't stop there. Job continued, wondering rhetorically whether we shouldn't also accept the bad along with the good from God (Job 2:10).

In other words, Job again affirmed God's sovereignty over our lives. This truth grounded Job in the immediate aftermath of his terrible suffering. From this spot, Job would not budge. That didn't mean, however, that Job understood what had happened to him.

Read 2 Corinthians 5:7. What did Paul say should guide our lives?

_____

_____

How does your previous answer correspond or contrast with the idea that Job should have been able to understand what happened to him?

_____

_____

_____

_____

 LET'S LIVE IT
Amid terrible suffering, Job's faith-filled response to God continues to serve as a powerful testimony to believers today. We can draw from this passage four important points to ponder that will prepare us for the day that may come when _we_ lose everything.

First, _everything starts with the kind of person you are._ Loss and suffering most often come upon us unawares. Therefore, we must spend time _daily_ cultivating our dependence on God, developing solid theology, living in obedience, and learning how to handle periodic tests.

What are you doing *right now* that is cultivating your dependence on God and developing your theology so you will be steadfast when tragedy hits?

_____

_____

_____

_____

_____

Second, *you don't know what will happen in the future.* We have no idea what tomorrow holds. But we do know the God who holds our future. And in that knowledge, we can rest.

How does Job's experience encourage you to see God as sovereign over your present and your future? What in your life reveals evidence of His sovereign care for you?

_____

_____

_____

_____

_____

Third, *warning: some people will give you wrong advice.* Just as Job's wife gave him bad advice, when tragedy strikes, some people will give us poor counsel—about God, the reason for our trials, and what we should do next. But as we stay rooted in sound theology and spend intimate time with the Lord, He will enable us to recognize bad counsel.

Think back to the experience you reflected upon at the beginning of this lesson. What advice did you receive? Was it good or bad?

_____

_____

_____

_____

What did you learn through experience that you can use to respond well if tragedy strikes again?

_____

_____

_____

_____

Fourth, consider right now, _how will you respond?_ Will you feel the freedom to grieve the painful occurrences in your life? Will you sense God's hand in the midst of your trial and respond with worship? Will you accept the fact that God _is_ in the midst of your situation?

Have you grieved the loss you mentioned at the beginning of this lesson — how? Has this experience driven you to worship, or has it taken you in a different direction? Describe your experience, and consider why you have responded this way.

_____

_____

_____

_____

Affirming God's sovereignty is easier said than done in the moment of crisis. On the lines below, write a prayer asking the Lord to ground you in solid theology, remind you of truth, and ignite in you a response of worship no matter what you may face.

_____

_____

_____

_____

Tens of thousands lost everything when Hurricane Katrina came raging onto the Gulf Coast. Others have lost everything at the _pop-pop-pop_ of gunfire or the doctor's grim-faced pronouncement: _terminal_. Job's experience remains vital in spite of the passage of millennia, because we continue to suffer and our trials drive us to ask questions about our Creator. Job's response to his suffering stands as a shining example for what we should do if we, too, lose everything. May his testimony provide you guiding light as you walk through your own dark valleys, not by sight but by faith.

What If You Are Being Stalked?

1 KINGS 19:1–14; JEREMIAH 17:9–10

 LET'S BEGIN HERE

Human depravity leads to every disturbing situation we can imagine. Sinful people think sinful thoughts, which if not restrained, result in sinful actions. This brings misery to others, which ranges from mildly aggravating to dreadfully painful. Chances are good that the majority of people you know are paying some serious consequences for someone else's unrestrained sinfulness. In James, we read,

> What is causing the quarrels and fights among you? Don't they come from the evil desires at war within you? You want what you don't have, so you scheme and kill to get it. You are jealous of what others have, but you can't get it, so you fight and wage war to take it away from them. (James 4:1–2)

Among the most unsettling situations we can endure are those occasions when someone "has it in for us," leading that person to intimidate, harass, or even threaten us. Stalking in particular creates an anxiety within us that makes us fearful as we attempt to cope. In this lesson, we'll briefly meet individuals in Scripture who were victims of stalking, and we'll look closely at Elijah's experience with Jezebel to learn how (and how not!) to handle this threat to our well-being.

LET'S DIG DEEPER

Diseased hearts yield dreadful results. Fallen humanity demonstrates the wickedness of our hearts in numerous ways—ways that all come back, at some level, to disobeying the great biblical commandments to love God and love others. When we refuse to love others, we refuse to take responsibility for them as human beings. We treat them as less than human.

Rowan Williams, an Anglican and the former Archbishop of Canterbury, brings this "taking responsibility" into sharper focus:

> To take responsibility is so to act and speak that the options of others are clarified, not controlled. . . . I become responsible when I can indeed "answer" for what is not myself, when I can voice the needs or hopes of someone other without collapsing them into my own. [1]

At its most basic level, stalking is seeking to control another human being through fear. It's an attempt to take the victim's voice. When it comes to stalking, then, depravity leads to dehumanizing results. This problem, which has been around for millennia and continues today, needs the benefit of careful, biblical guidance.

Have you ever been the victim of stalking or known someone who has? Describe the situation.

_____

_____

_____

_____

In what ways does a stalker's behavior treat the victim as less than human?

_____

_____

_____

_____

Identifying and Explaining the Problem

Stalking refers to contact from one person to another that is intended to threaten or spread fear within the victim. Everyone who stalks another person seeks some measure of control over the life of that individual. Stalking can involve a variety of different behaviors, including threats, harassment, following the victim, damaging property, and slander. The phenomenon of stalking is relatively common, though women suffer through stalking more often than men. Most who engage in stalking do so with specific knowledge of the victim, usually related to a failed relationship in business, romance, or some other arena of life.

The impact of stalking can be devastating for a victim, including loss of appetite and sleep, anxiety attacks, and even loss of employment, physical and sexual assault, or suicide. Stalking is a serious issue and a crime in most communities. If you or someone you know is currently being stalked, contact your local law enforcement for assistance immediately.

Meeting Some Victims in Biblical Times

While the word _stalk_ doesn't appear in Scripture, examples abound in both the Old and New Testaments. Gaining a sense of the scope of this activity in Scripture can help us be more attentive to its reality in our current context.

Each of the following Bible chapters includes an example of stalking. On the lines below each listing, record the stalker(s), the victim(s), and the results of the behavior, if mentioned.

Genesis 39

_____

_____

_____

Judges 16

_____

_____

_____

2 Samuel 13

_____

_____

_____

Acts 16

_____

_____

Focusing on One Man in Particular

One of the most famous examples of stalking in Scripture occurred when the wicked queen Jezebel threatened God's prophet, Elijah.

Read 1 Kings 19:1–14.

Elijah prophesied during the reign of Ahab and his Phoenician wife, Jezebel. When the marriage of the king and queen took place, idolatry increased dramatically in the land. This idolatry, overseen by Israel's leaders, led Elijah to pronounce a judgment of drought upon the Promised Land (1 Kings 17:1). Sometime later, Elijah gathered the idolatrous prophets and called upon them to bring down fire from heaven. When they failed, Elijah mocked them, called down fire from the true God, and had Jezebel's false prophets killed (18:19–40).

If Jezebel loved anything, it was the worship of the false god Baal that she brought with her from her years growing up in the Phoenician city of Sidon. She reacted to the news of Elijah's exploits with a crackling rage: "May the gods strike me and even kill me if by this time tomorrow I have not killed you [Elijah] just as you killed them [Baal's prophets]" (19:2).

The awareness that someone was stalking him left Elijah in a difficult position—one that he grossly mishandled. Rather than facing the situation and throwing himself upon God's mercy, Elijah ran to the far south of Israel, one hundred miles from where he received the threat. Elijah trekked out into the desert without consulting God, and when he did finally pray, he asked the Lord to take his life (19:4). This prayer for death is strikingly different from the life-sustaining prayer of faith he should have offered.

Read Matthew 6:11. How does the prayer in this passage contrast with the prayer Elijah offered in 1 Kings 19:4?

_____

_____

_____

_____

After praying, Elijah simply lay under a tree and waited to die. God could've lowered the boom on His prophet — Elijah had panicked and run far from his place of ministry, pursuing death rather than life. But instead, God sent an angel, provided Elijah with food, and prepared him to continue his journey to Mount Sinai (1 Kings 19:5–8).

Once at Mount Sinai, deep in the desert and far from any signs of civilization, Elijah came to the end of his journey. He was at a place so associated with God's presence that it was clear he had nowhere else to run. Elijah tried to explain what he was doing out in the desert, but God already knew. Elijah felt alone and threatened. And his feelings about his situation caused him to mishandle it. Rather than trust in the Lord as his deliverer, Elijah sought to deliver himself. And only when he had run as far as he could — can anyone get beyond God? — did Elijah understand his three serious failures.

First, *he immediately focused on the horizontal.* When Elijah heard his life was being threatened, he thought only about Jezebel's power. He imagined armies of idolatrous soldiers surrounding his home and tracking his movements. But Elijah gave no thought to God's power. Elijah's fear limited his thinking to his own abilities and those of other humans. The prophet couldn't get outside his head and the terrible imaginings he had about Jezebel's wrath.

Read Matthew 10:28. What did Jesus tell us we should fear?

_____

_____

_____

Read Matthew 10:29 – 31. According to this passage, why should God's people not fear?

_____

_____

_____

Second, *he completely miscalculated the situation.* Elijah believed he was alone. That was why he left Israel in the first place. Elijah sought out the loneliest places he could find to prevent himself from being captured by Jezebel. But on that desert mountain from which God had given the Law, the Lord visited Elijah in a gentle whisper (1 Kings 19:12). And in that moment, the prophet realized that he had never been alone. God had always been present. More than that, God told Elijah that seven thousand faithful people remained in Israel (19:18). Elijah had many more friends than he ever could have imagined. His focus on the limited view of the horizontal left him completely ignorant of God's wider view.

How does Isaiah 55:9 contrast God with humanity?

_____

_____

_____

_____

How could applying that truth have changed Elijah's approach to his difficult circumstance?

_____

_____

_____

_____

Finally, *he foolishly neglected his own personal needs.* Elijah wasn't resting. He wasn't eating. He wasn't drinking fresh water. Elijah had gotten so down on himself and his prospects that he stopped caring for himself. He was in a severely depressed state, and only a visitation from the Lord Himself was able to pull Elijah out of the doldrums.

LET'S LIVE IT

If you're being stalked, it's important to take the matter seriously. Contact the authorities, be aware of your surroundings, and be responsible with your life and the lives of those God has entrusted you with. As we do those practical things, however, we must do them with the right perspective—a perspective we should learn even if we never find ourselves in immediate danger. To gain that perspective, let's look at four truths we can learn from Elijah's experience of being stalked, his flight from Jezebel, and his ascent to the mountain of God.

First, *we are not immune*. Elijah was God's specially ordained prophet, and a stalker picked him out. If such a trial could happen to Elijah, it can happen to us as well. Therefore, we need to prepare ourselves for difficulties of all kinds. Trials should not surprise us when they arrive upon our doorstep.

Do you have the expectation as a follower of Jesus that He will keep trials from you? Why, or why not?

_____

_____

_____

_____

Second, *we're not bulletproof*. Let's not embrace the mistaken idea that we can handle difficult times on our own. None of us are superhuman. Whether it's stalking we face or another spawn of depravity, we will all be wounded in our lives. We will all need encouragement, nourishment, and refreshment.

How have you allowed other people to help you deal with the difficulties that have come into your life? If you have resisted help, take a moment to consider why and make a commitment to open yourself to the encouragement of the body of Christ.

_____

_____

_____

_____

Third, _we're not alone_. The experience of being stalked can make a person feel alone, vulnerable, and helpless. When threatened by Jezebel, Elijah believed he was the only faithful follower of God. In fact, Elijah believed that if he died, no faithful believers would remain to witness to the true God. Elijah was wrong. In the same way, we are not alone. There are always other believers working alongside us. We are not indispensable to God's work; He can and will make Himself known, with or without us. But we must remember that when He calls us to serve Him, even in dangerous situations, He will not forsake us, and nothing on this earth can take from us the eternal life He has given us. Such a perspective can help free us to serve fully and completely, without concern for our safety or preservation.

Have you ever wondered if there are other faithful believers working in the world? What truths from Scripture keep you from despairing over this issue?

_____

_____

_____

_____

Fourth, *we're not in charge.* Elijah believed he was in charge of his life, so he fled to safety. However, God reminded the prophet that only the Lord is sovereign—only the Lord knows all He has planned. When we face evil, we too must remember that the Lord is sovereign, and His purpose for us is greater than whatever wickedness comes against us. Rather than fleeing, we must ask the Lord to guide us in the right response.

Read Proverbs 16:9. How does this verse speak to God's role in your life versus your own perspective and plan?

\
\
\

Read 2 Timothy 1:7. What role have you allowed fear to play in your life? How can power, love, and self-discipline counter your fears and the wickedness you may experience?

\
\
\
\

Elijah's great victory over the prophets of Baal was followed by the greatest trial of his life. While still joyful about God making Himself known at Carmel, Elijah was caught up in Jezebel's threat and unprepared to properly deal with it. Whether through stalking or some other form of evil, we will each have those times when trials come upon us quickly, even on the heels of a great victory . . . for our great enemy, the Devil, is always waiting for an opportunity to devour us (1 Peter 5:8). May we keep at the forefront of our minds the lessons of Elijah's flight from Jezebel, so we may bear our trials with courage, faith, and an assured knowledge of who we are in Christ.

LESSON FOUR

What If a Longtime Friend Deceives You?

2 KINGS 5:5, 10–16, 20–27

LET'S BEGIN HERE

Few things sting worse than the realization that someone we trust has deliberately deceived us. At first, we find it almost too much to believe. It makes no difference who the deceiver is. It could be a trusted partner in business or a loyal individual we've known most of our lives. Perhaps it's the one we married, who promised to be faithful "til death do us part," or someone we admired and respected, such as a coach, teacher, pastor, or mentor. When we discover that person has deceitfully done something or said something damaging behind our backs, it's shocking and heartbreaking. David referred to this anguishing experience: "Even my best friend, the one I trusted completely, the one who shared my food, has turned against me" (Psalm 41:9). In this lesson, we will meet a man in Scripture on the opposite end of that equation, a man whom you've probably never met. Though unknown to most today, Gehazi was once a longtime, trusted servant of the prophet Elisha. For however long Gehazi served his master, he had apparently been both loyal and diligent. One tragic day all that changed . . . the day he replaced diligence with deceit.

LET'S DIG DEEPER

Healthy, thriving relationships require trust. When we trust one another, we give ourselves opportunities to break down the walls of isolation that so often surround us. Healthy relationships with those in our own homes, neighborhoods, offices, and communities allow love to be both given and received in the self-sacrificial way that Scripture commands. This mutual trust has the profound impact of grounding us within a network of relationships that sustain and mature us.

But when trust breaks down due to deception, more than relationship problems follow. The breakdown of mutual trust in relationships, seen so often in the contemporary Western world, isolates us from our churches, neighborhoods, and families. Worse, such deception has the potential to shake our faith at its very foundations.

Have you ever been deceived by a close friend? Describe the situation.

_____

_____

_____

_____

How did the relationship change after the deception was revealed? How has that experience impacted your life otherwise?

_____

_____

_____

_____

A Fresh Look at True Faithfulness

When Paul wrote to the Corinthian church for the first time, he described himself and his fellow minister Apollos as "servants of Christ and stewards of the mysteries of God" (1 Corinthians 4:1 NASB). With the terms _servants_ and _stewards_, Paul made clear the place of those who do the work of Christ in the church. Paul understood that Christ was the only head of the church, and the only position Paul, Apollos, or any other person ministering on Christ's behalf could claim was a position subservient to Jesus.

Servants and *stewards* bear out that second-tier position. The Greek term translated "servants" could also be translated "under-rower." The under-rower was a slave who powered the great Roman ships across the Mediterranean. Along the same lines, the Greek term translated "steward" can also be rendered "manager" and describes a housekeeper or butler—someone tasked with preparing meals for a family.

These terms indicate the service-oriented role that God's people play in making the church "go." God is looking for the faithful, not the famous. And yet, as we slave away at our tasks, the temptation to make ourselves advance, move on to a position of greater authority, or receive rewards for our service can captivate us.

A Miraculous Story of Physical Healing

That story of the church's under-rowers seeking to grasp something beyond their station is one we see throughout history and one that played out often in Scripture. One of the more pointed occurrences happened in the lives of Elisha and Gehazi.

 Read 2 Kings 5:1–16.

Naaman was a sick man. Though he had served well in the Aramean army, his strength and prowess couldn't prevent the onset of leprosy in his body. Against the ravages of illness, Naaman had no power. His humbled state became even clearer when a slave girl suggested to the mighty warrior that he visit a healer-prophet in her home country of Israel (2 Kings 5:2–3).

After visiting his own king and then the king of Israel, Naaman showed up on the doorstep of Elisha, Israel's godly prophet. Only in a meeting with the great prophet would the Aramean commander find healing. However, Elisha didn't operate according to Naaman's ideals or with the regard the warrior expected. When Naaman arrived at

Elisha's door, Elisha sent his trusted servant Gehazi to receive Naaman and to relay a message to the warrior: "Go and wash yourself seven times in the Jordan River. Then your skin will be restored, and you will be healed" (2 Kings 5:10).

After grumbling about his reception and instructions, Naaman eventually did as the prophet directed and then returned to Elisha's home to offer the prophet a gift. But Elisha wouldn't accept it, and Naaman headed back to Aram a healed man who could testify to the power of the Lord.

What was Elisha's goal with Naaman, according to 2 Kings 5:8?

_____

_____

_____

_____

How did Elisha accomplish that goal? (Hint: consider the specifics of Elisha's command.)

_____

_____

_____

_____

What does Naaman's initial angry response suggest about God's grace?

_____

_____

_____

_____

As we will soon see, Gehazi took advantage of Naaman for personal gain. Before we examine that part of the story, let's look for ways in which Naaman was at a disadvantage or in a position to be exploited. List at least three ways below.

_____

_____

_____

_____

A Downward Spiral of Shameless Deception

During the conversation between Naaman and Elisha in which Naaman had offered his gift, Gehazi had been listening. And when the commander and the prophet parted without exchanging any goods, the lure of silver led Gehazi to formulate a plan.

 Read 2 Kings 5:20–27.

Gehazi was Elisha's house servant, the under-rower who made things go. But in that moment when Naaman and Elisha parted, the desire to be in Elisha's shoes suddenly overcame Gehazi. He was stunned that Elisha didn't accept a gift and thought it only right and worthwhile that the household benefit from Elisha's work on behalf of Naaman. Of course, Gehazi completely missed the point—Elisha was merely the messenger of healing to Naaman. God actually did the healing, and as a result, Elisha felt no compulsion to exact a reward or even receive a gift.

But Gehazi had other ideas. He meant to capitalize on a humbled man. Gehazi sought personal gain from a stranger who was far from his home—a most grievous way to take advantage of someone else.

If that wasn't bad enough, Gehazi invoked the name of the Lord as he rationalized his desire to deceive (2 Kings 5:20). The result of his lie to the Aramean commander? Double the silver he had asked for . . . and more lies.

As with most lies, Gehazi's didn't end there. After returning home with the loot and hiding it, Gehazi was confronted by Elisha, who simply asked where the servant had been. In that moment, Gehazi had an opportunity to come clean, but he didn't take it. Instead, he lied to the face of God's prophet (5:25). The power of lies and the impulse to cover our shame is evident here. Gehazi lied to a man who communicated regularly with the Almighty. If anyone was going to know what Gehazi did, certainly it would have been Elisha!

When Elisha revealed that he did, in fact, know about the exchange, the prophet confronted the servant with a difficult question: "Is this the time to receive money and clothing, olive groves and vineyards, sheep and cattle, and male and female servants?" (5:26). Gehazi had usurped God's power to bless and taken on the mantle of one who doles out blessings to himself whenever he desires. In taking the gifts from Naaman, Gehazi attempted to step outside his God-given role and instead take on the role of prophet or even God Himself. In his mind, Gehazi—not the Lord—decided the time for blessing. This sinful deception made Gehazi and his family leprous, as they all bore the punishment for his hubris.

What do the following passages say about lying and its consequences?

Psalm 101:7

Proverbs 19:9

Colossians 3:9–10

What does Ephesians 4:25 suggest about the place of lying in the life of the believer?

What rationale does Ephesians 4:25 offer for telling the truth?

 LET'S LIVE IT

While Gehazi's account in Scripture is a tragic one, we need to recognize that, often, the best and most significant lessons we learn come out of tragedies. Sometimes we're on the receiving end of a deception, where someone else has lied to us. In those moments, we grieve over the brokenness in the relationship.

What exactly that grieving looks like is different, depending on the relationship. None of us are in a role like Elisha's; therefore, our response to deceit by a longtime friend will necessarily be different. But although the Bible doesn't reveal Elisha's feelings, human experience tells us that brokenness always yields sadness, and lies always produce consequences. For the sake of the relationship and our own selves, we must acknowledge that sadness, accept the consequences, and foster forgiveness. Sometimes forgiveness may go hand-in-hand with reconciliation. Other times, the relationship shouldn't be restored. Either way, we must ask the Lord to guide us and heal our hearts. And we must remember that He is a friend who will never betray us . . . and the example we should try to uphold.

In other words, we must be careful to not end up in the position of deceiver. We're often the simple servants—those under-rowers—making the church or the household or the office go. In these roles, we find ourselves in the place of Gehazi, facing similar temptations. We can't control others when they choose to deceive us, but we can learn two lessons from Gehazi's error as we seek to avoid a similar fate to his.

First, *leave no room in life for deception.* If you ask yourself before every decision, *What is the right thing to do?* you will better avoid deception. By simply prompting ourselves with that question, we'll remain attentive to the right things, which will push the wrong things out of our thoughts.

Second, *guard against rationalization.* If we are faithful to ask ourselves, *What's my motive?* we can give ourselves a way out of the trap of rationalizing our wicked thoughts and behaviors.

Think back to the experience you shared at the beginning of this lesson. Have you grieved the brokenness of that relationship? How?

_____

_____

_____

_____

Has that experience made you bitter and more likely to lie yourself, or has it taught you the importance of being honest?

_____

_____

_____

_____

How do you currently handle situations in which you believe you are the victim of deception?

_____

_____

_____

_____

In what areas of life or your relationships do you find yourself struggling with deception?

_____

_____

_____

_____

Think carefully about your motives in the major practices of your life — routines at home, office relationships, or church service. Are there places where your motives could be purer? Where?

_____

_____

_____

_____

Just as lies breed more lies, honesty breeds honesty. On the lines below, write a prayer, asking the Lord to set His truth in your heart, to help you see through others' deception, and to strengthen you to remain committed to being an honest person.

_____

_____

_____

_____

Deception hurts all of us at one time or another . . . and by the same measure, it tempts us. Some of us struggle with it on a daily basis. We often feel that the effects of any one deception are minimal, that they won't amount to much. But Gehazi's deception reminds us that our lies have effects—not just on us but on others as well. And while we might get away with one lie, as Gehazi did with Naaman, eventually our deceptions always catch up to us. Therefore, let us remember, regardless what hurts we may encounter, our faith is based on the one, true God . . . and with His empowerment, we can commit to living in truth in word and deed.

What If You Should Confront Someone in Sin?

2 SAMUEL 12:1–14

LET'S BEGIN HERE

Among the least-enjoyable yet important responsibilities of those who love the Lord is the task of confronting another believer who is living in deliberate disobedience. Scripture includes reminders that urge us to care for, warn, and help our fellow believers maintain their walks with Christ. Why? Because we're supposed to "set them straight"? No, of course not! We are instructed to do so because of our love for them. A popular description used today for carrying out this difficult yet essential responsibility is "tough love." Because we love our brothers and sisters, we care about them. Because we care about them, we must occasionally do what's tough: confront them. Even though it's difficult, even though the person being confronted may not respond as we hope, and even though we may be misunderstood, we must, nevertheless, do the right thing—in the right way—at the right time. Failing to do so is a violation of the biblical command, "If another believer is overcome by some sin, you who are godly should gently and humbly help that person back onto the right path" (Galatians 6:1). In the Bible, we see examples of this kind of "tough love," perhaps most notably from the prophet Nathan to King David. Nathan's is a model worth following today.

LET'S DIG DEEPER

Can't we all just get along? We've heard it before. We've probably even made the plea ourselves. We all appreciate the importance of peaceful relations. After all, we know that "getting along" makes life easier—simply by virtue of avoiding conflicts!

Sometimes, however, the "Can't we all just get along?" refrain asks for something other than true peace. In these cases, getting along becomes more important than getting it right. Standing for what's right gets lost in a strained "peacefulness" that no one really believes in. The effect of this cultural emphasis of getting along rather than getting it right has been dramatic. "Can't we all just get along?" has led some to have little concern for seeking out the foundational truths that should ground and guide our lives. Others believe such truths remain far from us, inaccessible in the middle of a confusing and uncertain world.

While the Bible makes clear the value of peaceable behavior (Romans 12:18; Hebrews 12:14), we understand that we must live within the tension that often arises between having stable relationships and being committed to the truth. Occasionally, our love for truth and for others requires us to engage in confrontation—to bring up difficult subjects that demand painful or embarrassing conversations. The fact is, we need people in our lives who love us and who love the truth enough to broach difficult subjects. For those of us who love the truth *and* love others, confrontation is a requirement from time to time.

Have you ever confronted another person about a difficult issue? Describe the situation.

_____

_____

_____

_____

Why do you think so many people avoid confrontation at all costs? List multiple reasons, if you can.

_____

_____

_____

_____

_____

Gaining an Understanding of Appropriate Confrontation

Confrontation—when practiced properly—is love in action. Our confrontation of another person should arise out of care for that person's welfare. When we see other believers who have placed themselves in dangerous positions or who have adopted harmful attitudes, our concern for their well-being should prompt us to confront them about their behavior.

To confront another person appropriately requires gentleness and humility. The apostle Paul advised the Galatian church to deal "gently and humbly" with the person overcome by sin, helping the sinner "back onto the right path" (Galatians 6:1). At some point, we've all wandered from the proper path. We've all experienced the shame that comes with sin. And as a result, we've all needed the firm but gentle response of others who are seeking our well-being. If we're honest, most of us would admit that we even wished for someone to give us that kind of help back onto the right path.

Appropriate confrontation involves gently reproving the sinner, but that doesn't include controlling that person in an attempt to make him or her like us. We want God's people to become like Christ and to pursue His ideals for their lives. Confrontation can easily end up as a veiled attempt to squeeze others into our molds. We need to avoid that temptation as we seek to help one another toward being conformed to the image of Christ (Romans 8:29).

Read John 16:8. What is the Holy Spirit's role, according to this passage?

_____

_____

_____

_____

If the Holy Spirit convicts of sin and every believer is indwelled by the Holy Spirit, what do you think is the role of the church—the body of believers—in confronting Christians' sin?

_____

_____

_____

_____

An Example of "Tough Love"

One of the most striking examples of appropriate confrontation we find in Scripture appears in the life of King David. After Israel had united under David and the army had much success beating back Israel's enemies, David became lax in his service to God and the people. Instead of leading his nation in battle, David remained home—while others led his army in battle. During one of his idle moments, the king saw a woman—Bathsheba—and sent for her. The resulting sexual encounter led to Bathsheba's pregnancy. David's attempts to use Bathsheba's husband as a cover-up failed, so the king ensured the man would be killed in battle. This dark period in David's life yielded a dramatic and confrontational response from God via His prophet Nathan.

Read 2 Samuel 12:1–6.

When Nathan arrived to speak with the king, the prophet spoke clearly and boldly. He didn't allow the difficulty of the moment—the fact that he was exposing the king's abhorrent behavior—to keep him from following through with the Lord's desire. In this moment, Nathan steadily carried out his task, reminding us that confrontation always requires courage.

Who sent Nathan to speak with David?

_____

What does that suggest about the quality of Nathan's message?

_____

_____

_____

_____

What in particular about the story do you think inspired David's fury?

_____

_____

_____

_____

A CLOSER LOOK
The Power of a Story

When he had to confront King David, Nathan told a story. Throughout human history, stories have served people in important ways. Stories have been used to teach history, to connect people to their communities or tribes, and to reveal the visible work of the invisible God in His world, among other things. When Nathan chose to tell a story about an oppressive and greedy rich man killing a lamb, his purpose was simple: to confront David with the truth of his moral failure.

In our current era, we tend to relegate stories to a place of "entertaining fictions." Seeing stories through this lens, however, is far too limiting for those of us who believe in the unmatched creative powers of our God. Seeing stories only as entertainment limits their ability to speak truth about the world, relationships, and God. Let's take our cue from Nathan and embrace the powerful ways stories can work in our lives. As the Bible makes clear, stories have always been, and will continue to be, a great deal more than a pleasant way to pass the time.

Read 2 Samuel 12:7–12.

When David grasped the wickedness of the rich man's greedy actions, Nathan seized the moment. Speaking forcefully as the king's fury erupted, Nathan told David, "You are that man!" (2 Samuel 12:7). Nathan delivered the harsh news as clearly as he had told the story moments earlier. David had received abundant gifts from the Lord, but he had cast aside God's prior graciousness and instead sought out his own lustful treasure . . . another man's wife. For this act, Nathan made it clear that David would be consigned to a life by the sword, a lifetime of turmoil within his own family, and the knowledge that these judgments would be public—not private like David's original sin.

Read 2 Samuel 12:9. What connection did Nathan make between God's word and David's deed?

_____

_____

_____

_____

What does this connection suggest to you about the importance of our deeds?

_____

_____

_____

_____

Though David's sin was private, the judgment was public. Why do you think God acted in that way?

_____

_____

_____

_____

📖   Read 2 Samuel 12:13–14.

Fear and resistance to the truth often precede confession. But that was not the case with David. Immediately upon realizing that he had been discovered, he confessed his sin. And God, through Nathan, offered David forgiveness, though not without consequence.

What consequence did David receive for his sin?

_____

_____

_____

_____

 ### LET'S LIVE IT
As believers who are a part of Christ's body, the church, we may find ourselves in a position where we need to confront a brother or sister. When we do, we need to remember these six guidelines for confrontation.

First, _let God lead_. Just as God led Nathan to confront David, so too should we wait on God to lead us when confrontation is needed. Realizing that confrontation is a natural part of life shouldn't prompt us to start confronting every time we see something amiss.

Second, _choose the right time very carefully_. Timing is crucial. Doing the right thing at the wrong time is the wrong thing. We need to consider timing carefully, through much prayer and thought. Only when the time is right should we confront.

Third, _speak the truth_. We must not use a confrontation as a time to exercise hyperbole or exaggeration. Instead, we need to stick to the facts, allowing the evidence of the wrongdoing to speak for itself.

Fourth, _use wise words_. We need to pray about the words we will use in confrontation and determine beforehand what we will say, allowing wisdom to season our thoughts. Though our words have a high chance of offending, we can rest easy when we know they are characterized by wisdom.

Fifth, _always offer hope_. Our goal is restoration, not condemnation. It's natural for the one engaged in sin to retreat from the light of truth. Therefore, we need to offer hope of renewed relationships and forgiveness.

Sixth, *leave the results with God.* We need to allow the Lord to do His work without feeling the need to wrench a decision out of someone.

Is there someone in your life whom the Lord is leading you to confront? If so, describe the situation and what you will do about it. If there isn't someone right now, how would you approach a situation that required confrontation, given what you've gleaned from this lesson?

_____

_____

_____

_____

What if you were the one to be confronted? What do you see in David's response that teaches you how to respond to confrontation?

_____

_____

_____

_____

❧

If it hasn't already, the need for confrontation will likely arise in your life. There's no need to look hard for opportunities—they will present themselves to you. But as you consider confronting a brother or sister in sin, do so prayerfully, carefully, and with much wisdom. And as you confront, always keep the hope of redemption at the forefront of your thinking—as God has forgiven you much, be prepared to forgive much of others. As God has welcomed you back into His family, be willing to welcome others back into full fellowship in the body of Christ.

What If Someone Kicks You When You're Down?

2 SAMUEL 16:5–14

LET'S BEGIN HERE

There isn't a single person reading these words who hasn't been hurt by someone else. All of us can remember someone who planned something, said something, or did something ugly or unfair to us. Because that's true, all of us can also name a person (or persons) we could blame for something! Recipients of mistreatment rarely forget how much it hurt. And if that mistreatment came at a "down time," when we were already feeling lower than a whale's belly and struggling to get back up, the offense hurt even worse. Because we've all gone through such harsh experiences, we should have no trouble understanding how David felt when, already at his lowest, he went through the misery of being pummeled with stones and debris and cursed in public. All of this hate came from a man named Shimei. Through this ugly and vile scene, we can learn much about how to endure mistreatment.

LET'S DIG DEEPER

Kicking someone who has fallen has long been taboo. In everyday life and on the battlefield, those who honor human life avoid the temptation to pile it on when a neighbor or a foe has fallen.

The theme goes back to some of the earliest literature in the Western world. In *The Iliad*, Homer's tale of the battle between the Greeks and the Trojans for the city of Troy, the two greatest warriors in the respective armies—Achilles and Hector—face off outside the city gates. After a furious battle, Achilles prevails over his opponent. And as the Trojan people look on—their hopes dashed with the death of their champion, Hector—Achilles straps the dead man to his chariot and drags him across the battlefield. The act dishonors Hector and leaves the people of Troy mourning their grievous loss (*The Iliad* 22).

Human beings have been telling such stories throughout history. The dignity of human life inspires most of us to show respect for the dead and the downtrodden. But there are times when selfishness, short-sightedness, or just plain wickedness drives some to cross the line and refuse to respect another image-bearer—another human being—in a low position.

Have you ever been kicked when you were down? What were the circumstances?

_____

_____

_____

_____

How did you respond?

_____

_____

_____

A Painful Reminder of Sin's Consequences

The Bible is filled with accounts of people whose grief in their lowest moments was compounded by the negativity of others. King David, spoken of so highly in Scripture for the bulk of his life, struggled through a similar experience. No doubt Saul's famous murderous pursuit of young David would qualify, but another story provides a brief but compelling picture of how to respond to those who kick us when we're down.

The low point of David's reign came as a result of his adultery with Bathsheba and his subsequent murder of her husband, Uriah. When God's prophet Nathan pronounced judgment upon David, he made it clear that the king would experience difficult times in the coming days. Though David confessed and God forgave, the days after Uriah's death were certainly some of the king's lowest.

A litany of tragedy struck David and his family after the king's sin was exposed. The child conceived in the adultery died (2 Samuel 12:19). One of David's sons, Amnon, raped his half-sister, Tamar (13:14). Amnon's half-brother, Absalom, waited two full years and then took revenge for the rape of his sister by gathering a group of men to murder Amnon (13:29). Absalom then led a rebellion against his father, forcing David to flee Jerusalem and find safety elsewhere (15:14).

Talk about a humble state! David had ascended to the heights of leading God's people, as God's chosen and faithful servant. But the king's sin led to a downward spiral that left him lower than he had been since his days as the youngest son keeping his father's sheep. And yet, even in this lowered state, David discovered that there were those who would happily trample him further.

How would you say James 4:6 speaks to David's situation as it has been described so far?

_____

_____

_____

_____

Read Psalm 138:6. Now look at the beginning of Psalm 138. Who wrote this psalm? What in David's life might he have connected with this verse?

A Brutal Account of Shimei's Hatred

Public figures receive lots of attention, not all of it pleasant. As King David fled Absalom and moved out of Jerusalem, he found himself the focus of such unpleasant attention . . . and he encountered an enemy he never knew he had.

 Read 2 Samuel 16:5–8.

Family bonds run deep—so deep that sometimes when a beloved relative falls, those close to that person respond defensively against those who've benefited from the loved one's demise. When Saul, the former king of Israel, succumbed to the sword and bloodshed covered his family, David ascended the throne. Later, after the new king had begun to pay the price for his sins with Bathsheba, he traveled to the village of Bahurim. Along the way, a man of Saul's clan named Shimei heard that David was nearby and took advantage of the opportunity to unleash some pent-up anger upon Israel's anointed king. As the rage poured forth from Shimei, David had to have known instantly that the man had no idea what had actually happened between Saul and the young king. Although Saul had sought to take David's life, David had repeatedly refused to kill Saul, even when given prime opportunities to do so (1 Samuel 24, 26). Shimei's attack had no basis in actual fact. To make matters worse, Shimei approached David at a particularly difficult time for the king. The disgruntled relative reared back to kick David when he was already down. Who could guess what the king might do?

What was Shimei's attack on David based upon?

_____

Read James 1:19. How do you think this piece of wisdom might have helped Shimei?

_____

_____

_____

_____

  Read 2 Samuel 16:9–14.

Among David's small traveling party was a warrior called Abishai, who had earned his place alongside David for his loyalty as well as his prowess on the battlefield. Abishai had once felled three hundred of the enemy with only a spear! When Shimei attacked, the response of hot-tempered Abishai is one we might expect from a battle-hardened soldier: "Let me go over and cut off his head!" (2 Samuel 16:9). Abishai had no interest in standing by while some stranger insulted God's anointed. In his fury, Abishai mirrored Shimei—both men took offense and let their words get away from them. Shimei and Abishai embodied the aggression of their viewpoints. Shimei threw rocks; Abishai threatened beheading. David, by contrast, chose magnanimity.

In the face of Shimei's obvious anger and Abishai's furious response, David told the latter to back off. The king understood what it was like to be surrounded by death. David had lost a son and another was trying to kill him, while Shimei had just lost a huge number of his own clan. Death's sting spreads into the lives of the survivors. Shimei was understandably hurting and angry, and he reacted to the presence of the man he believed to be most responsible. Shimei met David when he was already in a low state, and no incident in the king's life better illustrates his humility than his generous response to Shimei. A closer look at that response yields four insights for us today.

First, *David silenced and restrained any kind of violent retaliation.* In the heat of an attack, we often strike back with physical or emotional violence. The apostle Paul exhorted us, however, to avoid revenge and instead allow God to take up our defense and handle justice (Romans 12:19).

Second, *David took the high road.* David allowed his attacker to have his say. The harm done by Shimei's words and rocks came nowhere near making Abishai's offer of beheading necessary. David stayed on higher ground and allowed Shimei his moment of grief.

Third, *David refused to defend himself.* David could have fired back at Shimei. He could have answered the attacks with an avalanche of verbiage. But David resisted the temptation, because he understood where Shimei's anger was coming from. David's restraint came from his humility—from his willingness to consider others better than himself.

Finally, *David left justice in the hands of the One who is always and perfectly just.* Effectively, this meant that David allowed Shimei to continue his rock-throwing and ranting. Indeed, Scripture says that the attacks went on so long that David and his party grew weary of them (2 Samuel 16:14). Nonetheless, David refused to retaliate and instead trusted in the Lord.

Consider the crucifixion of Jesus. How does the passion and suffering of Jesus mirror what we see in David in this story?

_____

_____

_____

_____

What does David's and Jesus's willingness to endure suffering tell us about godliness?

_____

_____

_____

_____

 A CLOSER LOOK
"I'm Offended!"

In our day, everyone is ready to proclaim offense at one thing or another. Some take offense at hearing certain words, while others become distressed by particular behaviors. Whatever the infraction, it's become almost faddish to say, "I'm offended!"

David had a perfect opportunity to take offense. Shimei, David's critic, threw stones at the king of Israel and had the nerve to call him "a butcher" and "a hellhound" (2 Samuel 16:7 MSG). A man of David's power and position would not have been questioned had he ordered Shimei to prison or even execution. But instead of taking offense and pursuing the path of punishment, David absorbed Shimei's angry words and eventually answered them with forgiveness (19:16–23).

David's response to his harsh critic provides a way forward for us as believers living in a culture that relishes taking offense. It shows us that absorbing the hits of foolish people trumps reacting to them or retaliating.

We should take note of two final observations from this story of David and Shimei. First, *success and popularity can make you proud or they can keep you humble.* David was the most famous man in all Israel. And though he had been chased from Jerusalem, he could still have leaned on his pride as he dealt with others. But David refused to take that path and instead thought of himself in a lowly, humble state, in direct contrast to his success and popularity.

Second, *being kicked when you're down can paralyze you or prompt you to keep going.* David chose the latter, and his traveling party continued their journey. Kicks while we're down might tempt us to give up, but David's life reminds us to keep going.

 LET'S LIVE IT
In those times when someone delivers a kick while you're down, take to heart these four practical suggestions.

First, *ask God to give you a tougher hide.* We need not be so sensitive and easily offended. Staying close to the Lord in prayer will help us to stay strong and assured of our identity in Christ in the midst of attacks.

Would you describe yourself as having a tough hide? Why, or why not? How does 1 Peter 2:20–25 encourage you in this area?

_____

_____

_____

_____

Second, *remember that God is ever aware and engaged even if He is silent.* God is altogether sovereign. He knows what He's doing and when He's going to do it. Keeping that in mind will help us to persevere through the difficult moments.

Third, *rely on God's grace when you deal with people like Shimei*. God gives to us from His abundance of goodness and grace. We need to trust that He will provide for us when others attack us.

Fourth, *find comfort by resting in God's mercy*. When attacks come, we need somewhere to rest our weary bones. We find that oasis in God's mercy.

Read Psalm 25:15–17. How might this passage encourage you when someone kicks you while you're down?

_____

_____

_____

_____

_____

_____

We've all experienced the pain of taking a hit when we're already in a humbled state . . . and many of us have also experienced the regret of lashing out or responding to hurtful words with angry words of our own. Let's follow David's example of grace in the midst of attacks and allow the Lord to direct our steps as we seek to model godliness in our lives—in even the most difficult circumstances.

What If You Need a Second Chance?

ACTS 13:2–5; 15:36–41

LET'S BEGIN HERE

Each of us can remember a time when we failed to do something we said we would do. We started strong. We had every intention to follow through. And others were relying on us to stick to our commitment. To make matters worse, we gave them our word that they could count on us. And then, somewhere along the way, our good intentions got sidetracked. Circumstances became difficult. And we failed to follow through. Those who counted on us were disappointed in us, and we felt guilty. At that point, two things likely happened: 1) having lost trust in us, some of the disappointed people determined to never rely on us again, and 2) having had time to think about how we would handle things differently, we longed for a second chance. The Bible includes several examples of people who blew it and later longed to be reinstated. Peter needed a second chance after he was disloyal the night of Jesus's arrest (Mark 14:66–72). Jonah needed a second chance after he ran from the Lord's command to carry His message to Nineveh (Jonah 1–2). The adulterous woman needed a second chance to prove her character (John 8:1–11). Esther needed a second chance to respond to Mordecai's plea to help their people (Esther 4:10–17). And as we'll learn in this lesson, young John Mark needed a second chance to prove himself to Paul and Barnabas after deserting them on their first missionary journey (Acts 13:13; 15:37–38).

LET'S DIG DEEPER

The movies have long been a home for second chances. Few examples have become more iconic than the classic Frank Capra film *It's a Wonderful Life*. The story is familiar to most: a failing businessman named George Bailey—played by Jimmy Stewart—thinks that ending his life will benefit his family in the long run. With help from an angel, George sees a vision of what his town would be like if he had never existed. The disturbing vision reveals a town in turmoil, and George receives a second chance to go back and make his business right.

The affecting conclusion speaks to the deep, human yearning for getting another shot at life after a moment of weakness. At the end of the film, George's gratitude can't be hidden as his forgiving and supportive family and community surround him. This story of receiving a second chance has been told time and again because it's a story that people everywhere relate to.

Have you ever needed a second chance? Describe the situation.

_____

_____

_____

_____

Have you ever had the opportunity to grant someone else a second chance? Describe the situation.

_____

_____

_____

_____

Familiar Situations in Everyday Life: Second Chances Are Often Needed

All of us have needed a second chance. As toddlers, we only learned to walk after falling down more times than our parents could count. And yet, after the umpteenth fall, our parents didn't throw their hands in the air and declare that we would never get it. Instead, they stood us right back up and encouraged us to try again.

As we grow older, our circumstances become more complex, but our need for second chances remains the same. Excessive anger and underhanded manipulation in our marriages leave us in need of another shot time and again. A harsh word to a child or a thoughtless deed at church prompts us to cry out for another opportunity to live well.

Where would any of us be without second chances from virtually everyone in our lives? The chilling answer is hard to swallow: we would all be isolated and alone, cut off from community with others. Second chances are vital, a truth that Scripture makes clear time and again.

An Example from the First Century: John Mark with Paul and Barnabas

The early church spread quickly through the Mediterranean region. As churches sprang up in cities, God often called their teachers onward to bring the gospel to people who had not yet heard. Case in point: Antioch.

 Read Acts 13:4–5, 13–14.

Saul, also known as Paul (Acts 13:9), and Barnabas were two prominent teachers in the Antioch church whom God called to minister in other places (13:1–2). But these two men didn't go alone. They brought young John Mark, "who was also called Mark" (Acts 12:12 NASB), as an assistant—one who would take care of many details associated with traveling. However, Mark was not just any young man. He had grown up in Jerusalem in a home that had been a refuge for the church in its earliest years. Furthermore, Mark was family—a cousin to Barnabas. Mark had every advantage from the perspective of heritage, making him a perfect companion for these two teachers on a mission for God.

Read Mark 10:44 – 45. What does this passage reveal about service in relation to Jesus's ministry?

_____

_____

_____

_____

How might Jesus's perspective in Mark 10 have been helpful to John Mark as he headed out with Paul and Barnabas? How might it be helpful today to a person starting out on a mission for God?

_____

_____

_____

_____

After ministering on the island of Cyprus, the travelers sailed for Asia Minor and landed in a port called Perga. There John Mark left the group (Acts 13:13). We don't know the exact circumstances of his leaving. Did Mark tell Barnabas or Paul? Or did the young assistant just sneak away in the night? There are a number of possible explanations for Mark's behavior.

The trek ahead in Asia Minor would have been difficult. Though Perga was at sea level, traveling further into Asia Minor would've meant a grueling, mountainous journey that promised physical strain. A second theory is that John Mark suffered homesickness. He was further from home than he had ever been, and after weeks or even months on the road, he may have grown tired of their nomadic lifestyle. Another reason might have been the way that the group dynamics had shifted—what had started out as a Barnabas-led group had become one led by Paul. Mark may have struggled with the switch and felt the need to cut ties.

What other legitimate reasons can you think of for John Mark to have left the party?

_____

_____

_____

_____

How would you feel if a valuable assistant left you in the middle of an important project?

_____

_____

_____

_____

Read Acts 15:36–41.

In his record of the event, Luke told us nothing of Paul's immediate reaction to John Mark's leaving. However, we do know how it affected Paul later. Sometime after their return to Antioch, Paul and

Barnabas explored the idea of returning to the churches they had started on their previous journey. Both men were excited by the prospect, aside from one thing: John Mark. Barnabas wanted to bring along his cousin again; Paul would have none of it.

These two magnificent servants of Christ couldn't agree about the practical matter of who to take as their assistant. Perhaps Barnabas wanted to do a favor for his young cousin. More likely, Barnabas saw an opportunity to give John Mark more seasoning, to allow the young man to show himself trustworthy in a grown-up situation.

Paul, on the other hand, felt betrayed and deserted. The apostle to the Gentiles thought that Mark had compromised the mission of the gospel and that by breaking from the mission party he had broken away from what God wanted him do in the world. Where Paul looked at the principle of the matter, Barnabas focused on the person involved.

Read the following verses penned by Paul. Describe their teaching.

Galatians 6:9

_____

_____

_____

_____

2 Thessalonians 3:13

_____

_____

_____

_____

2 Timothy 2:12

_____

_____

_____

_____

How do you think Paul's experience as a traveling missionary corresponds with his teaching on the Christian life in the verses above? Consider specifically his experience of being deserted by John Mark.

_____

_____

_____

_____

Who was right in his response to John Mark? Was Paul right to reject the young man? Or was Barnabas right to include John Mark for the next journey? Scripture doesn't say, so it's up to the perspective we choose to take. Certainly, John Mark had failed at the level of the principle, and Paul had every right to wish for a different assistant on his next journey. However, if placed in John Mark's shoes, we would all have loved a second chance and been eager to prove our trustworthiness. Both Paul and Barnabas had a point, and they each felt strongly enough about the issue to go their separate ways. Although their split had its own level of tragedy, it also allowed them to double the range of their ministry (Acts 15:39–40).

LET'S LIVE IT

From time to time, we're all going to find ourselves in John Mark's shoes. When that happens, we must first be honest—with ourselves and with those we've failed. We must admit our failure, ask forgiveness, and consider what motivated us to back out of our commitment and how we can grow through the failure and avoid making the same mistake twice. We must also practice humility, understanding that we've angered and hurt someone who counted on us and that regaining that person's trust will be difficult at best, impossible at worst. Whether we're given a second chance by that person or not, we each need to thank God for the second chances He gives us and ask Him to help us be faithful and resolved as we move forward.

Think back to your answer to the first question in this lesson. Have you grown through that failure? How?

_____

_____

_____

_____

Just as we'll all stand in John Mark's shoes from time to time, we'll all also slip on Paul and Barnabas sandals. People *will* fail us. And when that happens, we must decide what to do. How do we determine—amidst others who might disagree—what to do with the individual who failed? Here are four guidelines to help you navigate those treacherous waters and make the right choice.

First, *when in disagreement, work hard at seeing the other point of view.* We tend to get locked into our own way of seeing things, which makes it difficult to communicate with those who disagree. We can only respond well to others when we first understand their view.

Second, *when both sides have excellent support, seek a wise compromise.* At certain times, we'll run into issues with multiple good solutions. In the case presented in Acts 15, there were good reasons both to take and to leave John Mark. Paul and Barnabas could have sought out a compromise about giving John Mark a second chance. Instead, they took the lesser route of separation.

Third, *when conflict persists, care enough to work it through rather than stomp it out.* When we disagree over whether or not to give a second chance, we need to commit to finding a solution, no matter how hard it seems. That might mean many conversations over a period of time. It will definitely require kindness, patience, and coolheadedness to work through areas of disagreement. But the resulting solution will be worth it.

Fourth, *when you can't reach a resolution and you must disagree, try not to become disagreeable.* We've all experienced times when we've worked an issue over and over and simply cannot come to a conclusion. We need to be able to part ways with others without holding grudges. We must recognize that despite our disagreements, God can use both parties in great ways.

Do you disagree or have you recently disagreed with someone about offering a second chance? Describe the situation.

_____

_____

_____

_____

How do the four guidelines above speak to that situation?

_____

_____

_____

_____

❧❀❧

God has always been a God of second chances. There will be times when we find ourselves asking for another chance, knowing we don't deserve it. There will be other times when we're asked to give someone else a second shot . . . or a third one or fourth one. Sometimes we'll be called upon to grant that wish. Other times, like Paul, we'll feel compelled to stand on principle and trust that the second chance will come to that individual some other way. Whatever the case, let's commit to being humble recipients of grace and conduits for second chances just as our God is for us.

What If You Struggle with a Permanent Disability?

2 CORINTHIANS 12:1–10

LET'S BEGIN HERE

Paul's second letter to the Corinthians is his most autobiographical. It is in this letter that the apostle of grace wrote with unguarded vulnerability. In every great life there are depths which others observe and admire but into which precious few are given access. Paul certainly qualified as one of the greatest who ever lived, and his story leaves us intrigued over what gave him such depth of maturity, breadth of wisdom, height of contentment, and capacity for grace. This section of Scripture in 2 Corinthians, however, pulls back the curtain of Paul's life, allowing us to see one of the major secrets of his greatness. Amazingly, it wasn't his great giftedness, great intellect, or great tutoring by great mentors; it was the realization of his own inadequacy brought on by the excruciating pain of a permanent disability. Paul called his disability "a thorn in my flesh" (2 Corinthians 12:7). The downside of this "thorn" was the awful torment it brought. The benefit was that it kept Paul from being self-sufficient. The pain he endured forced him away from self-serving pride and toward an all-important discovery: "When I am weak, then I am strong" (12:10). Thanks to this thorn, Paul found that God's grace was sufficient, which led him to embrace a truth that most people overlook, namely: "Power works best in weakness" (12:9).

LET'S DIG DEEPER

There's a fine line between believing in one's own abilities to accomplish a task and an arrogant attitude that develops into self-sufficiency. Almost everyone wants to be able to contribute to his or her family, church, and community. Individuals thrive when they have some talent or skill through which they can serve others. Churches and communities thrive as a result of having those kinds of individuals in the population.

However, an ever-present danger remains for the talented and skilled: the tendency to speed off on the freeways of pride, arrogance, and self-sufficiency. Often, the talented and skilled overestimate their abilities and think themselves capable of more than is actually true.

Do you take pride in being self-sufficient? What does *self-sufficient* mean to you?

_____

_____

_____

_____

What role do you think the community (church, neighborhood, city) should play in the life of each person? How does a person's belief in self-sufficiency impact or limit the community?

_____

_____

_____

_____

_____

Those Who Appear Self-Sufficient

Someone who is self-sufficient seeks to live without assistance from anyone. The truth is, no one is actually self-sufficient, and those who attempt to be find themselves alienated from family and friends, lonely, depressed, angry, and distant from the loving God who wants us to rely on Him. Yet, despite these emotional and spiritual dangers, individuals continue to pursue self-sufficiency with abandon. And though no one ever truly achieves it, there are many who *appear* to be completely adequate in and of themselves. We can often find these folks in three groups.

First are *the highly intelligent*. These have quick minds. They test well. They can comprehend on the fly and deliver timely, witty remarks. These people seem clever and self-confident, thus support-ing the idea that they really are self-sufficient.

Second are *the greatly gifted*. Some among us are tremendous ath-letes. Others possess artistic or musical skills that leave us in wonder. As these people produce their works of art and achieve feats of athleti-cism, they appear completely adequate to the uninitiated observer.

Third are *the deeply religious*. This group lives in the realm of the "ultra-holy." Their knowledge of Scripture dwarfs our own. Their clar-ity in prayer never ceases to move us. This religious ability gives off an air of spiritual depth that provides a sense of their sufficiency.

Do you know any people in the groups above? What qualities make them appear self-sufficient?

_____

_____

_____

_____

Read 1 Corinthians 4:7. What does this text remind us about the sufficiency of others' talents and skills? Of our own?

While it's easy to see people in the groups above — or even ourselves — as self-sufficient, we must resist the temptation. Why? Because when it comes to self-sufficiency, all of us — no matter how talented or skilled or well-esteemed — eventually have to admit that we are dependent creatures. We depend on God for the very gifts we rely on. We depend on others for the support and wisdom and helping hands we all need to get through the mundane and the extraordinary. When we fail to make this recognition about ourselves or others, we compromise the community we share with both God and humans.

A Classic Example: Paul

God wants us all to come to grips with the reality of our brokenness, of our dependent condition. One of the greatest examples of this perspective comes to us from the pen of the apostle Paul.

Paul's religious resumé was impeccable. If anyone was adequate in and of himself, it would've been him. Paul came from the right family; he was taught by the right people. Everything seemed to set him on a higher plateau. Second Corinthians 12, however, paints a more detailed portrait of the apostle — a portrait painted by the apostle himself with light and shadow, bright colors and dim.

📖   **Read 2 Corinthians 12:1–4.**

First of all, *Paul was a man of unsurpassed privileges.* Sure, he had the proper upbringing and training. But his privilege extended far beyond heritage and community. Paul had received a special revelation from the Lord—"caught up in the third heaven fourteen years ago," he called it (2 Corinthians 12:2). God has not brought many into the throne room. This was a unique privilege for Paul, even among the apostles.

Paul knew his heavenly experience was special, but he only mentioned it because the church at Corinth had questioned his qualifications as an apostle. In other words, Paul had kept this striking fact to himself in order to keep the focus of his teaching on the Lord.

How does Ephesians 2:19–20 describe the role of the apostles?

_____

_____

_____

_____

Given your previous answer, what unique reason do you believe the Lord may have had for revealing Himself in a special way to Paul?

_____

_____

_____

_____

Read 2 Corinthians 12:5–6.

Second, *Paul was a man of uncommon humility*. If it wasn't enough that Paul spoke directly about this revelation only in this specific context, he then made it clear that he had no intention of boasting about this brag-worthy experience. Paul's concern was instructive: he didn't boast because he didn't want people to give him credit for more than he actually did. A fanciful story about receiving revelation directly from heaven might have encouraged people to inflate Paul's work, to tell tall tales about him, and to increase the sense that he had some special power within himself to do the Lord's work. Paul wanted no part of that; he was content with giving all credit to the Lord.

Read Galatians 1:15–18, a passage that details Paul's movements right after the incident he described in 2 Corinthians 12:2. How did the apostle handle being "caught up to the third heaven"?

_____

_____

_____

_____

Read Galatians 2:20. Whom did Paul say was responsible for his life and work? How does this verse inform the humility we see in Paul in 2 Corinthians 12:5–6?

_____

_____

_____

_____

Read 2 Corinthians 12:7–8.

Paul had the great privilege of receiving direct revelation from God, yet he remained humble. How? *Paul was a man of inescapable pain.* The apostle told the Corinthian church that he had received a thorn in the flesh. In other words, Paul had in his life some kind of painful trouble that he could not get rid of. He never made clear the exact nature of the pain, but he did reveal that this thorn helped keep him humble.

The thorn — or stake, as it is sometimes translated — indicates a debilitating or disabling kind of pain. Paul had to grapple with this reality even though he repeatedly asked God to remove it from his life. And it wasn't as if Paul's motive for asking for relief was selfish — he wanted to continue his rigorous travel schedule of sharing the gospel throughout the Mediterranean region!

What is the promise of Revelation 21:4?

_____

_____

_____

_____

How should that promise impact a Christian's perspective on enduring pain today?

_____

_____

_____

_____

Read 2 Corinthians 12:9–10.

Because Paul was humbled by his pain, he was able to do the kind of work that God wanted him to do. This reality reveals that *Paul was a man of paradoxical power*. When Paul asked God to remove the thorn, the Lord made it clear that His power works best in weakness. The Lord worked more powerfully in Paul because of the apostle's weakness. Indeed, God even told Paul that His power would be perfected in weakness. In other words, the reality of God's power and its effectiveness in the world comes about through the weakness of human beings.

What does this all mean? It means that we who follow Jesus and His apostles should expect that God will work most powerfully in the midst of our weaknesses. It does not mean that we may not petition God for relief or that He will not give it. But it does mean that instead of allowing our pain to breed resentment or hiding our weaknesses in shame, we should show others how God uses us to accomplish His purposes despite, or even because of, those difficulties.

LET'S LIVE IT
We all have disabilities — ways in which we don't function as we were designed. We all know the pain of thorns in the flesh. And as a result of our weaknesses, we all have prime access to God's grace working in our lives. So what should we do when we find ourselves disabled in some way?

First, *look up*. God is sovereign over all His creation. He is not surprised by our disabilities. He is not surprised by our limitations. We can trust Him to care for and comfort us in the midst of our struggles and to work through us — by His grace — in spite of them. This perspective will allow us to avoid being overburdened by the weaknesses in our lives.

Second, *look within*. God wants us to be joyful in spite of our brokenness. When we see that He continues to work in us even though we are broken and have struggles, we can take joy in His faithfulness to do what He has promised He would do. He perfects His power in the midst of our weakness.

Finally, *look beyond*. We need to see our circumstances with a view that stretches beyond the immediate. God is doing a work in us, one that He has promised will conclude in a world without sorrow or pain or death. Such hope will help us continue on despite the thorns.

In what ways do you consider yourself disabled? Don't think merely of physical handicaps but also in a broader sense that includes your spiritual, mental, and emotional brokenness.

_____

_____

_____

_____

How have you witnessed God's working through your brokenness and pain? Give specific examples.

_____

_____

_____

_____

What does your recognition of your own disability suggest about the common "ideal" of self-sufficiency?

_____

_____

_____

_____

God works through the thorns in our lives. In this sin-stained world, where we all struggle with disabilities and weaknesses, God sees fit to use those things to magnify His name in the world. Some of us have easy-to-see disabilities. Others of us harbor weaknesses within. Whatever the case, we need to strive to see those disabilities in a purer light, one that recognizes that God graciously continues to work in the midst of this fallen world.

What If a Person Is an Unrepentant Troublemaker?

ROMANS 16:17; TITUS 1:4-7; 3:3-11

LET'S BEGIN HERE

Just as a family works best when there is harmony and cooperation, so does a congregation. No parent enjoys dealing with children who misbehave, but ignoring them or giving in to them are not good options. The same is true in the family of God. Throughout the history of the church, there have been those who stirred up trouble and caused dissension. Such troublemakers will always exist. To keep the unity that is so vital in a healthy church, those who habitually and persistently sow discord must be confronted, dealt with, and encouraged to repent. Unfortunately, there are always a few who refuse to repent even when confronted; these call for stronger measures. Admittedly, these situations represent one of the more difficult and unpleasant aspects of ministry and the Christian life.

LET'S DIG DEEPER

Throughout the last five hundred years, the Christian church has increasingly splintered. Tens of thousands of new denominations have sprouted up over doctrinal differences and practical preferences. While God has always appreciated diversity within the church (just look at the wide variety of people who came to believe in Christ during Pentecost!), He also wants to see us retain our unity.

In our modern, fragmented context, the contemporary church struggles more than ever to prioritize unity. When difficult people create problems in their churches, others immediately have numerous options for simply removing themselves from the situation and relieving the tension. The very presence of multiple churches—which initially seems so nice for the "church shopper"—becomes a burden to Christian churches trying to hold on to unity.

The reality of church life is simple: we will encounter difficult people. We will have disagreements with others in the church. And we will struggle with how to handle those troublesome situations. Jesus knew this when He prayed that Christians might remain as one (John 17:11, 21–22). Therefore, we need to do the hard work of figuring out how to remain unified with those who we find distasteful or hard to endure.

In your experience in the church, have you come across people who were difficult to relate to? Describe one or two of them.

Now consider yourself. What in particular about yourself do you think might make it difficult for another church member to be in relationship with you?

Two Realistic Facts

While we understand that the church is always going to have people in it who frustrate us and try our patience, clarifying how things *really* are in the church can be helpful. Two facts are undeniable.

First, *those who lead are very big targets.* Any leader worth his or her salt carries a big target on his or her back. Leading means that troublemakers will eventually find you.

Second, *those who follow are sometimes very stubborn.* For whatever reason, there are those in the church who like to make others miserable. Remarkably, these troublemakers often wreak their havoc while retaining a good-natured sheen.

A Quick Review of Chronic Troublemakers

As long as there has been sin, there have been rebels. As long as there has been leadership, there have been those who have fought against leadership. Let's take a look at some of the troublemakers we find buried in the pages of Scripture.

Early in the biblical narrative, the siblings of Moses—Miriam and Aaron—criticized God's chosen leader (Numbers 12:1). Apparently, the woman Moses chose for his wife wasn't up to their standards, which led them to believe they were at least as qualified for the role of prophet as Moses was (12:2). Further, we see in this passage that the motivation behind their grumbling largely seems racial, as the text mentions the woman's Cushite origins not once but twice in close succession. Casting judgment on Moses because his wife was a Cushite—a person from the Upper Nile region who would likely have had dark skin—led the siblings to overestimate themselves and led God to bring His judgment upon them (12:9).

Throughout the Bible, other troublemakers raised their difficult heads. Achan disobeyed God and refused to follow the Lord's appointed leader, Joshua (Joshua 7). Judges 21:25 reminds us that Israel had a period of time during which it was full of rebellious-minded individuals. David had numerous troubles with his sons Absalom and Amnon, while Nehemiah and Daniel were stalked by their opponents. In the New Testament, Jesus dealt with frustrating Pharisees and smug Sadducees, while Paul and other apostles constantly had to warn churches against false teachers. Near the end of Scripture, the apostle John mentioned Diotrephes, a man who sought to be first among the local Christians. Diotrephes loved having pre-eminence in the church and refused to welcome the apostle John and others who sought to be a part of the church community.

Indeed, troublemakers were everywhere.

Scan Job 1–2. What kinds of troubles befell the man?

_____

_____

_____

_____

When Job's three friends arrived, how did they initially respond (Job 2:11–13)?

_____

_____

_____

_____

Scan the next several chapters of Job. How did Job's friends make trouble for him? (For an example, see Job 6:14–15.)

_____

_____

_____

_____

How do you think this affected Job? (Scan some of Job's responses, such as Job 6:1–30 for ideas.)

_____

_____

_____

_____

A Firm Warning

Since troublemakers are prone to stir the pots of our churches, it shouldn't surprise us that the leaders around at the beginning of the church offered stern warnings to Christians in danger of being led astray by troublemakers. The apostle Paul offered one such warning to the church at Rome.

 Read Romans 16:17–18.

As Paul concluded his majestic letter to the Roman church, he wanted to make sure that the people would remain on stable ground as a community. This meant watching out for those who would seek to create fissures in their church community by teaching something contrary to the apostles' doctrine. We have to observe the divisive behavior before we can do anything about it. What did Paul suggest we do? "Stay away from them" (Romans 16:17). In other words, when people begin to influence our churches and teach in ways that are contrary to the good news about Jesus and the teaching we have received from the apostles, we need to protect our communities from those false teachers by keeping our distance.

But why? Paul made it clear in the following verse: "By smooth talk and glowing words they deceive innocent people" (Romans 16:18). The people who teach things contrary to the message of Christ and His apostles are deceivers. The Evil One wants to use these people to get God's people off track and to keep others from the Lord altogether. Deceivers use every trick they can think of to take advantage of us. Therefore, we must keep our distance.

How did Paul describe false teachers in the following verses?

Acts 20:29

_____

_____

_____

Galatians 4:17

_____

_____

_____

How would you react to people who exhibited the above qualities?

_____

_____

_____

_____

A Specific Example

Sometimes, the best way to receive guidance through a problem is to look to a real-world example. When it comes to examples of people who have had to deal with troublemakers, the Bible has given us a great one in the person of Titus—Paul's protégé and church planter extraordinaire on the island of Crete.

 Read Titus 3:8–11.

The churches of Crete were sorely in need of stability. The answer? Strong leadership. Titus had been tasked with finding elders for fledgling groups of believers on Crete so they might remain in line with the teaching they had received from Paul. Ultimately, Paul's concern for the people of Crete was that they would continue to follow God, faithfully doing good in every area of their lives (Titus 3:8). Strong leadership would help ensure that they would hold fast to the teaching that they had received.

Paul wanted Titus to insist on certain teachings in order to ensure that the Christian churches would continue doing good (Titus 3:8). Read Titus 3:4–7 and describe the content of this particular teaching.

Why do you think holding on to the teaching you just described would lead people to devote themselves to doing good?

Paul's advice didn't end at telling Titus what to hold on to. He also offered him some advice about what to let go of. Specifically, Paul told Titus to avoid foolish discussions, quarrels, and fights (Titus 3:9). Paul understood that for the churches to survive they had to remain unified. Achieving long-term unity meant that the Christians on Crete had to understand which fights were worth it and which fights were a waste of time.

Paul was wise enough to know that although Titus and other faithful believers might avoid useless fights and arguments, others in the community would not. Paul's advice on this issue is crystal clear: anyone causing division among God's people should receive two warnings, and then they should be removed from the church. Unity, then and now, is more important than keeping the "pot-stirrers" around.

What was Paul's reason for considering divisive people as individuals outside the community? (See Titus 3:11.)

What do you think following Paul's instruction about divisive people would look like in your current church context?

LET'S LIVE IT

When it comes to dealing with troublemakers in the church and remaining unified, we need to remember one thing only: *we are each the secret to having a healthy, wholesome, and happy church.*

In other words, it's up to each of us to love others well. In some cases, when people come among us and stir up dissension, we as a church need to keep our distance; that in itself is an act of loving well. By protecting the vulnerable from those who seek to harm them, we exercise the same kind of love that Jesus offers us in our weakness. Adopting a simple, three-phrase statement can help you discern when to call upon those protective instincts: "In essentials, unity. In nonessentials, liberty. In all things, charity."

While all that we do should be motivated by love, we know that our unity should rest in the essentials of the faith—those things which have been handed down from Jesus and His apostles. For all other issues, we can allow for disagreement while continuing to live in unity with our fellow believers.

How have you dealt with church troublemakers in the past?

_____

_____

_____

_____

How would you evaluate your actions in light of Paul's teachings above from Romans 16:17–18 and Titus 3:8–11?

_____

_____

_____

_____

What is the most significant thing you think you can do to avoid being a troublemaker in your church?

_____

_____

_____

_____

❧

No one likes troublemakers. They require us to expend inordinate amounts of energy to protect those we care about and keep our communities healthy. However, we cannot ignore the reality of troublemakers. We need to be able to hold a firm line when the unity of the body of Christ is threatened while still remaining in fellowship with those who disagree with us on the nonessentials. Only when we strike the balance between these positions will we keep our churches healthy and vibrant.

What If You Talk Too Much?

MATTHEW 15:10–20; JAMES 3:1–12

LET'S BEGIN HERE

Honestly, do you talk too much? Do you find yourself saying, "I shouldn't say this . . ." and then going right ahead
and spilling it out? Do you promise to keep information
shared in confidence, only to leak it a few days (or even a few hours)
later? Do you spend too much time filling the air with words, yet say
very little worth hearing? Worse, do you speak against others behind
their backs and then say something completely different to their faces?
Are you prone to outbursts of sarcasm, insults, and profanity . . . and
then, only a short time later, to bursts of flattery, compliments, and
insincerity? If these sound like your habits, you're like the majority.
Verbal restraint is rare — in fact, *consistent* verbal restraint is almost
nonexistent. No wonder the Bible has so much to say about getting
our mouths under control! Few disciplines are more important or
necessary than learning to bridle our tongues.

LET'S DIG DEEPER

Distressed by hypocritical Christians and lackadaisical
commitment within the church, some early Christians
decided to set up self-sustaining communities devoted
explicitly to the pursuit of holy living. One such early Christian,
Benedict of Nursia, wrote what became a very influential set of rules
to govern the behavior of those who lived within these communities.
The rules consisted of a number of practical matters — including
scheduled times of community Bible reading and guidelines on how
to be obedient and humble.

One of the keys to humility, according to Benedict, involved controlling the tongue: "The ninth step of humility is that a monk controls his tongue and remains silent, not speaking unless asked a question, for Scripture warns, *In a flood of words you will not avoid sinning.*" [1] Benedict didn't believe that his community should be completely silent. Rather he believed that his community should be a place of disciplined speech, a place whose inhabitants used words to turn the focus toward learning about and connecting with others. Benedict understood the potential for wickedness in our tongues, so he figured out a way to use them positively.

Have you been hurt by those who have spoken too much? Describe the situation below.

Have you hurt others by speaking too much? Describe the situation below.

Jesus States the Source of Our Problem

While most of us see the reality of the problem with our tongues, we often seek remedies that treat the symptoms of the problem rather than driving straight to its source. Jesus clarified that source as only He could, using straightforward language that reveals our fundamental condition in all its broken-down glory: "The words you speak come from the heart—that's what defiles you" (Matthew 15:18).

Jesus understood that our problem with saying the wrong thing begins with the heart, rather than the words themselves. Often we believe that whatever pops into our heads needs to be spoken. However, we need to make sure those words pass through a filter that determines which words are beneficial, helpful, and good. If we have words that fall outside that realm, we should keep those words to ourselves and instead spend time seeing to the transformation of our hearts.

And where does transformation come from? It comes to believers from the indwelling Holy Spirit, who works in us over the course of our lives to conform us to Jesus Christ. As we are attentive to that process, we can expect transformed hearts and, as a result, more success controlling our tongues.

James Addresses the Control of Our Tongues

The reality of our fallen hearts means we need to pay attention to our tongues (words), recognizing that we need to exercise self-control in that area of our lives. The apostle James offered some of the most pointed teaching on taming the tongue in the whole of Scripture.

 Read James 3:1–2.

In verse one of the third chapter, James began his treatment of the tongue with a warning to those who speak to others—specifically, to those who teach. Not many should aspire to the role of teacher—for those who teach, James said, will be judged according to a higher standard. But why?

First, teachers must speak the truth. Teachers stand before a group of people to deliver information. They must check their facts and do their homework in order to ensure that the words they speak are indeed true.

Second, teachers affect many lives beyond their own. Teachers guide students in their lives. The Christian teacher, who talks to people about the Bible and theology, has great potential to do harm to others simply by teaching things that aren't true.

Third, teachers are expected by God to live according to what they teach. Students can test the words of their teachers against the lives of those teachers. If they don't match, the resulting hypocrisy can be incredibly damaging to individual students and to the church as a whole.

In James 3:2, James broadened his warning about words. Whom did he include in this part of the warning?

_____

_____

_____

James said if we control our tongues, we will be "perfect." What does this suggest about the power of words?

_____

_____

_____

_____

DOORWAY TO HISTORY
Don't Desire to Teach?

In the early church, a number of the most significant Christian teachers took seriously the warning found in James 3:1. Far from aspiring to their offices, Christians such as John Chrysostom and Gregory of Nazianzus sought to avoid positions of leadership in the church. These men felt the weight of responsibility associated with teaching in the church, so it was only through the fervent pursuit of others that men like John and Gregory came to hold church offices.

One of the more well-known of these instances involved Augustine, the famous North African theologian. Whenever Augustine heard of an open leadership position in a city, he made himself scarce, avoiding the city until the position had been filled. However, during the time that the position of bishop was open in the city of Hippo, Augustine had a friend there who fell ill and stood in need of prayer. Unable to deny his friend, Augustine traveled to Hippo. While Augustine prayed in the city's church, the people crowded around him and called for him to accept the office of bishop. Only under such duress was Augustine persuaded to take on the position.

A story like this helps us see the contrast between how ancient Christians responded to the warning in James 3:1 and how some Christians do today. Unlike some leaders who climb church ladders today, these ancient believers weren't pursuing the plaudits of others. Rather, they saw themselves as deeply responsible to God and His people, and they feared (in the most appropriate, Proverbs 1:7-sense of that term) to tread upon the ground of leadership without the proper reverence.

After James broadened the warning to include all people in James 3:2, he transitioned into direct teaching on our use of language. Three principles about our tongues become clear in this passage.

 **Read James 3:3–5.**

First, *the tongue is small but powerful.* James offered three examples of small things that control powerful things: a horse's bit, a ship's rudder, and a spark that starts a fire. Each of these vivid, concrete images reveals to us the power of the little muscle in our mouths that we call the tongue.

With such great power at our disposal, we who control the tongue need to see the importance of keeping it bridled. We shouldn't overlook our tongues because they're small or because they sit hidden in our mouths. Rather, the tongue's power should cause us to pay extra attention to it in order to ensure that it's used properly.

What is it that James said the tongue can do? (See James 3:5.) Why is this something we should approach with care?

_____

_____

_____

_____

What is the danger in overusing our tongues, according to Proverbs 10:19?

_____

_____

_____

_____

Read James 3:6–8.

Second, *the tongue is necessary but dangerous.* Notice the strong metaphor James used in his discussion of our speech: "The tongue is a flame of fire" (James 3:6). We all know that fire can be used for good purposes—who doesn't like a bit of food from the grill or a warm home? But we also know flames can do great damage if they have opportunity and fuel to thrive. Both fire and tongues require attention and boundaries.

Indeed, our tongues can be evil, death-bearing instruments. This potential for wickedness rests in our tongues because our hearts are fallen. Though God has redeemed His people and indwelt us with Spirit, the power and presence of sin remain within us. We need to fight the impulse to rebel with our tongues. If we don't trust in the Lord's ability to transform our hearts and do the diligent work of filtering our speech, the results will be devastating.

Think about the list of creatures James gave in 3:7. Which one do you think would be most difficult to tame?

_____

Now compare that creature to your tongue — do you see your speech having the same potential for wildness that you see in that creature? Why, or why not?

_____

_____

_____

_____

How do you think you would go about taming your tongue?

_____

_____

_____

_____

Read James 3:9–12.

Third, *the tongue is helpful but inconsistent.* We know the terrible power that rests in our tongues, but we need not forget that the tongue is also helpful. It's using our tongues consistently for good that's the challenge. Too often, we offer praise to the Almighty and curse the pinnacle of His creation in the same breath!

As we seek to make good use of our tongues, we need to consistently and intentionally speak in ways that are helpful and bring healing to others. Our words should be characterized by life and renewal, never death and destruction.

Read Proverbs 31:8–9. What kinds of words should we be speaking in light of this passage?

_____

_____

Consider the promise of God's kingdom, of the eternal life God's people will spend with Him. How do the words of Proverbs 31:8–9 relate to that blessed promise?

_____

_____

_____

_____

LET'S LIVE IT

Having thought about the roots of our wickedness and the dangerous and helpful potential of our tongues, we can draw out two practical applications that we should never forget.

First, *you will never regret restraining your tongue.* Often, we get caught up in emotion and say things we shouldn't. Given the task, we all could remember a recent time when that very thing happened. When we hold back our words and avoid saying something motivated by the emotion of the moment (rather than by truth, necessity, or kindness), we allow ourselves the space and opportunity to really consider what we say before we say it.

Second, *apologize for the times you have failed to restrain your tongue.* Obviously, this is the more difficult task of these two applications, simply because we have spoken out of turn so many times. But for all of us, there are those specific times burned in our memories when we know we spoke out of turn and should apologize for the rashness of our speech. Start with making it right with those individuals. When you apologize, express your regret. Reveal your sorrow. And ask for forgiveness.

Are there people from whom you need to seek forgiveness, due to an out-of-control tongue? List their names on the lines below.

_____

_____

_____

_____

What will you say when you approach these individuals?

_____

_____

_____

Use these last few lines to offer a prayer to the Lord — for forgiveness for the ways you've misused your tongue, for commitment as you prepare to repair relationships, and for a continual transformation of your heart that will help you as you move forward with a controlled tongue.

_____

_____

_____

_____

The power of the tongue often surprises us. Its ability to tear down is well known. But we need not forget that it has the power to encourage and build up as well. As we consider the kinds of words we speak, we must remember to focus on speaking words that build up and bring life. By remaining focused on the positive potential of our words, we can actively work against the wicked tendencies so deeply rooted within ourselves.

What If Your Boss Is Unfair and Disrespectful?

GENESIS 1:1, 27, 31; 2:1–2, 15; 3:1, 4, 10–19; 1 PETER 2:13–21

 LET'S BEGIN HERE

If you're currently employed or were once engaged in the workforce, you understand what it means to answer to someone in authority over you. Since that's true, you need no convincing of the value of a great boss . . . one who is caring, equitable, and respectful. In many ways, the relationships we have with those in authority over us determines whether we enjoy (or don't enjoy) our work. It's safe to say that all of us are aware of how difficult it is to carry out our responsibilities when the one we work for lacks thoughtfulness, understanding, and ethical integrity. This is intensified if the boss claims to be a Christian but does not carry out his or her responsibilities as a Christian should. When essential characteristics are lacking in those at the top, our otherwise enjoyable jobs (or callings) can become unpleasant and unsatisfying tasks, which create a challenge to our attitudes. Being caught in the midst of that awkward dilemma forces us to ask: *How should I respond to this kind of leader?* To discover the surprising answer to this question, we must first examine the truth about our work as set forth in Scripture.

 LET'S DIG DEEPER

When many people hear the word *work*, their countenances drop, their shoulders slump, and their blood pressures rise. For a few, the mere mention can provoke negative reactions normally reserved for war criminals. Other people have so little invested in their work that its mention leaves them completely unaffected. For these, the prospect of being laid off is merely a pointer to move on to the next job. In other words, we have a deficit in our contemporary world—a deficit of good and careful thinking about work.

As believers, we need a robust theology of work. That might sound intimidating, but in reality it's pretty simple: we need to think about work in a way that's consistent with the way God thinks about work. Too many of us have gotten caught up in the rat race or have bought into the lie that our lives should be filled with as much recreation as possible. As Solomon found out nearly three thousand years ago, work isn't the answer to all our problems (Ecclesiastes 2:21–23), but neither is work an enemy that needs to be eliminated from our lives.

How would you describe your attitude toward work?

_____

_____

_____

_____

How do you think God views your work?

_____

_____

_____

_____

Clarifying Comments about Our Work

How can we think biblically about work? Many of us have heard from the pulpit so little about work that we wouldn't know where to turn first to find out what the Bible says about work. To get a foundational sense of what God intended work to be, we should consider the accounts of creation and the fall in the early chapters of Genesis.

The Bible says that when the Lord finished creating the world, "he rested from all his work" (Genesis 2:2). And when the Creator fashioned Adam, He placed him "in the Garden of Eden to tend and watch over it" (2:15). God expected Adam to work, even during this era of innocence and perfection. And why would God expect such a thing, except that God Himself was a worker!

However, due to sin, our work has become difficult (3:17–19). We struggle under the weight of responsibility in ways that Adam never would have if he hadn't sinned. And that struggle often causes us to loathe work. However, when we do, we forget that God created us to work and that work is fundamentally a good gift from God. As we consider our thinking about work, four statements can help us move toward a more well-rounded vision.

First, *Jesus Christ is Lord over all of life.* There aren't certain parts of life over which Jesus is not Lord. Wherever we are, whatever God has given us, the work we do happens under the authority of Jesus. Therefore, the Lord cares immensely about what each one of us does every day. That includes our work.

Second, *life is not divided into the categories of sacred and secular.* The work before us is from God. When we work, we need not try to divide what we do into sacred and secular, into "godly work" and "everything else." Whether we're filling a spreadsheet with numbers, digging a drainage ditch, or coaching a high school tennis team, we do our work unto the Lord. In this way, we are no different than the minister who prepares the sermon or the song leader who prepares the music—we each have specific works that God has called us to do.

Third, *the nature of your work is good, not evil.* When God set up the world, He made it a place for working. This world, which God called "good" as He created it, was made to contain workers. Work was a part of that good world. The presence of sin doesn't make work evil; it makes work hard.

Finally, *the way you do your work is a direct reflection on the One who called you to it.* Therefore, when we don't work hard, we reflect poorly on the Lord who called us to that work. We need to take care that we work well.

Read Proverbs 13:4. What wisdom does this verse offer about work?

_____

_____

How do you think a lifestyle of hard work reflects God well? What is it about God that corresponds to the hard worker?

_____

_____

_____

_____

Roles of Christians in the Workplace

Now that we know how to think well about work, we need a clear view of what that looks like in practice. Some passages in Paul's letters can give us clues about how to live out a proper theology of work.

 Read Colossians 3:17, 23.

In Colossians 3, Paul gave a specific command about which parts of our work we should do in honor of the Lord: "whatever" we do, we do it as representatives of Jesus. In other words, we should allow our status as followers of Jesus—rather than our particular feelings at any one moment—to determine how we work. If we were really to work this way, it would revolutionize our lives. We would stop dreading our jobs and start placing our focus on *how* we work (diligently, intelligently) rather than on our particular jobs. Living out this perspective will not mean that we will avoid difficulties in our jobs, but rather that our responses will be more in line with Christ.

A CLOSER LOOK
Slaves = Employees?

Many in this day and age interpret the "slave" passages in Ephesians and Colossians by substituting the word *employee* for *slave*. The intent is often honorable—the preacher is looking to find a way to apply the passage in a contemporary context when none of his listeners are slaves. But when we come to such passages, it's helpful to remember a couple points.

First, *slave* and *employee* are not equivalent terms. Slaves have no control over their destiny. They have to direct their steps in the way that their masters direct. This is true with modern-day slavery, and it was true in the first-century world of Paul's letters. An employee in the contemporary world is, therefore, nothing like a slave at the most fundamental level.

Second, we must be careful not to skip over the important context of biblical slavery passages. Paul consistently advocated for a kinder and more harmonious relationship between slaves and masters. Further, there are times when Paul seemed to indicate that freedom from slavery would be preferable (1 Corinthians 7:21; Philemon 15–16). That said, in our modern world, we know that slavery is detestable and to be avoided, whereas working relationships and work itself are good things we should foster.

However, none of this means we shouldn't apply the "slave" passages to a modern-day work context. We can certainly draw lessons about relationships where one person holds some power over others from these "slave" passages. But we should do so while taking care to remember the significant differences between slaves and employees and between masters and employers.

Read Colossians 3:22. What are three lessons from this verse that we can apply to a modern-day work environment?

_____

_____

_____

_____

What do you think Paul expected to see as a result of workers obeying the above commands?

_____

_____

_____

_____

Read Colossians 4:1. What command in this verse could be applied to our modern-day leaders in the workforce?

_____

_____

_____

_____

What do you think Paul expected to see as a result of leaders obeying the above command?

_____

_____

_____

_____

How does the reminder that leaders have a Master in heaven contribute to the kind of relationship between leaders and workers that Paul advocated?

_____

_____

_____

_____

When Christians Serve Leaders Who Are Unfair and Unkind

What about those occasions when we find ourselves in the difficult situation of working for someone who doesn't treat people well? How should we respond? The apostle Peter spoke directly to this pertinent issue.

Read 1 Peter 2:13–21.

When Peter wrote his first epistle, wicked Nero reigned in Rome. Even still, Peter advocated that Christians "respect all human authority" (1 Peter 2:13). Why would Peter do such a thing? Certainly not because of the quality of the leader, but because of the quality of Peter's God. The Lord wants us to be respectful of *all* authority in our lives. When it comes to work, we don't have to believe our bosses are inherently good people who don't make mistakes or naturally avoid wicked desires. We can recognize the fallenness of these men and women, even as we give the respect due them.

**How far did Peter extend the principle of accepting the authorities —
such as that of bosses (1 Peter 2:18–20)?**

_____

_____

_____

_____

**To whom did Peter point as the example we should follow as we seek
to embody this principle of accepting authority? How is this example
pertinent in the workplace?**

_____

_____

_____

_____

 LET'S LIVE IT

When it comes to working with difficult bosses, most
often we need to resist our natural inclinations, lest we
fall into sin ourselves. As we have seen already, God's
expectation of our respect for authority doesn't hinge on the authority's character. And God's expectation of our doing diligent, thoughtful
work doesn't change when our bosses are unkind. What should we do
if our bosses are unfair and disrespectful? Scripture's answer is simple:
work as unto the Lord.

However, there are occasions when we must resist the directions
of those in authority. A few practical lessons will help direct our
thoughts in these situations so that our lives become characterized by
Christlike perseverance.

First, *resist when you are called upon to do what is wrong*. The Lord does not expect us to engage in sinful behavior. Daniel was commanded to worship an idol, and he resisted. In the same way, if our bosses introduce us to some kind of fraudulent or otherwise illegal activity, we should avoid it.

Second, *resist when your conscience is being violated*. The book of James tells us that it is sin to know the right thing and avoid doing it (James 4:17). We each have a conscience, and we need to be attentive to its promptings.

Third, *resist when innocent people will be affected by your doing evil*. Of course, we shouldn't be engaging in evil actions to begin with, no matter who is impacted. But sometimes, only the presence of the innocent can awaken our consciences enough to change our course.

What kind of working conditions are you under?

_____

_____

_____

_____

Given the insights in this chapter, how can you better approach your working life, whether or not you have to deal with a difficult boss? Be specific.

_____

_____

_____

_____

_____

_____

Are there certain attitudes about work in general that you need to change? What are they, and how will you seek to change them?

_____

_____

_____

_____

❦

Our thinking about work has got to improve. When it does, our work will improve too. We've had it all wrong, buying into the popular narrative that it's okay to moan and wail about jobs and bosses and responsibilities. However, we must recognize that both work and authorities come from God, and as such both are worthy of our respect. May you use this lesson as an opportunity to better appreciate the work that God has given you.

What If You Were to Die Tonight?

LUKE 16:19–31

LET'S BEGIN HERE

Death. The topic is strewn with the litter of fear, igno-rance, and superstition. For many, death is viewed as an unsolvable mystery, a vague departure from this life that leaves those who remain disillusioned and confused. Others hold erroneous beliefs about death, including soul sleep, reincarnation, and the possibility of making contact with the spirits of the departed. For most, it's one of those socially unacceptable subjects—something nobody wants to discuss. Therefore, it surprises many that, rather than ignoring the subject and skirting the issues surrounding it, the Bible—like no other book—faces death head-on. It offers reli-able, God-inspired information that answers most of our questions and calms our fears. In fact, the Bible not only addresses heaven, the death-related subject everybody wonders about; it also speaks openly and authoritatively about the death-related subject most choose to deny altogether: hell. During His earthly life and ministry, Jesus taught clearly about both heaven and hell. In the passage we'll consider in this lesson, He brought both to the surface in an amazing story we cannot forget.

LET'S DIG DEEPER

In *Jayber Crow*, a pastoral novel about a small-town barber, Wendell Berry writes this poignant passage on death:

> One of your customers, one of your neighbors (let us say), is a man known to be more or less a fool, a big talker, and one day he comes into your shop and you have heard and you see that he is dying even as he is standing there looking at you, and you can see in his eyes that (whether or not he admits it) he knows it, and all of a sudden everything is changed. You seem no longer to be standing together in the center of time. Now you are on time's edge, looking off into eternity. And this man, your foolish neighbor, your friend and brother, has shed somehow the laughter that has followed him through the world, and has assumed the dignity and the strangeness of a traveler departing forever.[1]

When we allow ourselves to think about it, we realize the imminence of someone's death is something of a beautifying mystery. Seeing another person—even one who has proved himself or herself foolish—face the prospect of death brings us to a moment of reckoning. We see that person in a new light. We sense the tension created by impending death. And we feel the sadness of losing someone, which prompts us to grow in our appreciation for life.

And yet, most of us somehow manage to continue on, missing the opportunity to grow and thinking little of our own deaths. We take what comes in life, making changes here and there. And all the while, death remains removed from our thoughts and, therefore, a mystery.

Have you had a close encounter with death, such as an accident, illness, or loss of someone close to you? Describe the situation.

_____

_____

_____

_____

How has this brush with death impacted your view of God and His work in the world?

_____

_____

_____

_____

How has this brush with death impacted your view of yourself and how you live?

_____

_____

_____

_____

An Understanding of the Life Beyond

To unshroud the mysterious nature of death, it helps to answer a few simple questions about what happens when people die. As you read through this section, please refer to the chart on page 123.

To understand what happens when we die, we need to first understand the origins of death. After God created man and woman in the garden of Eden, He forbade them from eating the fruit of the Tree of the Knowledge of Good and Evil (Genesis 1:26–28; 2:16–17). However, they ate and brought death into the world (Romans 5:12). Death and sin have always been companions.

When people die, others typically bury the bodies in the earth. People's souls—the immaterial part of us—have different destinations, depending on whether or not the deceased was a follower of Jesus. The souls of Old Testament followers of, or believers in, the true God were sent to Paradise and brought to dwell with Christ at His ascension. The souls of those Christ-followers who have died since Jesus came to earth, died, resurrected, and ascended go directly to be with the Lord in heaven (2 Corinthians 5:8). The souls of all believers—those dead and those still living—will rise with their resurrected and/or glorified bodies at the rapture and then—after the seven-year tribulation on earth—will return with Jesus as He sets up His earthly millennial kingdom. After Jesus reigns on earth for a thousand years (Revelation 20:1–6), all believers—in glorified bodies and souls—will live with Him eternally in the new heaven and new earth (Revelation 21–22).

However, those who don't believe in Jesus have a different destiny. The souls of nonbelievers are sent to a place of torment. In this terrible place, they too await the resurrection of their bodies. But instead of life, nonbelievers will receive a judgment that will send them to the second death: eternal punishment in the lake of fire (20:14–15).

What is the promise of 2 Corinthians 5:8?

_____

_____

_____

_____

What kind of response do you think a believer should have to a verse like this?

_____

_____

_____

_____

A Story of Two Who Died

During His ministry, Jesus told a story that gives us insight into the nature of death, pulling back the curtain to reveal something of the great mystery of life beyond life.

Read Luke 16:19–23.

Jesus's story introduces us to two contrasting figures—a rich non-believer and a poor believer. The poor man, Lazarus, sat outside the rich man's gate, waiting and hoping for a few scraps of food to sustain him. The rich man—who goes unnamed in the story—lived in opulence and comfort. While dogs licked the poor man's open wounds, fine clothing of the most luxurious kind covered the rich man.

Eventually, Jesus said, the poor man died and was carried "to be with Abraham" (Luke 16:22). In other words, the man's spirit went to dwell in the place where Abraham—one of the original followers of the true God—also dwelt. When the rich man died soon after, he did not go to be with Abraham but rather to a place of death and torment (16:23).

What do the following verses have to say about the rich and the poor?

Proverbs 14:31

_____

_____

_____

Isaiah 58:10

_____

_____

_____

What implications about a person's relationship with God can you draw from whether or not he or she follows the guidelines in the verses above?

_____

_____

_____

_____

     Read Luke 16:23–26.

We need to make an honest assessment of the place of future torment. In Jesus's story, the rich man begged the poor man for relief—a role reversal for the two men from their earthly lives. Abraham told the rich man that although he had everything he wanted in his earthly life, he now would dwell in anguish. While on earth, perhaps the rich man held the same types of ideas that nonbelieving cynics hold today. Those in this group often make four common rationalizations in attempt to ignore the reality of future torment.

First, the cynic says, *"Hell will be a relief! All my hell and suffering are taking place in this life — on earth."* This perspective, while optimistic about future bliss, ignores the weight of the truth revealed in Jesus's story. The pain and pleasure we know on earth do not indicate what kind of life we will live after death, nor do they even begin to match the pain and pleasure available in hell and heaven. The rich man didn't go to a place of anguish because he enjoyed a luxurious lifestyle, and the poor man didn't go to be with Abraham because he had suffered so much. Jesus's story, rather, reveals that those who live for anything other than God are headed for a torment after death unlike any on earth.

Second, the cynic says, *"All this stuff about hell and suffering after death is all based on imaginary fears!"* By focusing on the fears of those who believe in eternal torment, this cynic essentially skirts the issue by critiquing not hell but those who believe in it. The concrete imagery of the passage in Luke, however, makes it clear that torment isn't simply a fool's fear. Those who dwell in eternal torment will experience it consciously: the rich man could *see* Abraham, he could *feel* anguish, he could *speak out*, and he could *remember*. These experiences are hardly the fears of imagination.

Third, the cynic says, *"I'll be there with all my friends. We'll be fine. I'm not going to be alone!"* While the cynic may know plenty of friends headed for hell, there will be no great party. Jesus's story reveals quite the contrary. While in torment, the rich man thought about those who were no longer with him — his five brothers (Luke 16:28). Further, there's the fact that Lazarus could not cross over from his place of comfort (16:26). Isolation is part and parcel with torment.

Finally, the cynic says, *"After I'm there a while, I'll get out. Someone will pray me out of that place."* Although this is a popular belief, it has no biblical support. Jesus's story, in fact, directly contradicts this, as Abraham stated that no one can cross from one place to the other. Those who go to torment have nothing else to look forward to . . . except more torment.

Scan once more through the story of the rich man and Lazarus. Did the rich man ever ask to leave his place of anguish?

_____

What might this suggest about those who find themselves in torment?

_____

_____

_____

_____

     Read Luke 16:27–31.

The rich man did ask Abraham to act on behalf of his living family, begging the great Patriarch to send a resurrected Lazarus to warn them about the reality of this torment. Abraham responded, however, that the Word of God is far better than a sign. Revelation is superior to miracle. In a day when many look for miracles, this story reminds us that all the testimony we need is written for us in this magnificent book—the Bible.

Read 2 Timothy 3:16–17. What is Scripture useful for?

_____

_____

_____

_____

LET'S LIVE IT
Three significant lessons arise from the study of this story in Luke's gospel.

First, *God's written Word is the most important evidence a person on earth can examine.* Nothing beats the Bible in lighting the way to the Lord—not supernatural occurrences, not miracles, and not visions. Many, many people have been convinced of the truth of God's good news by simply being exposed to God's Word.

Second, *God's written Word is the most compelling information to prepare us for the life beyond.* Seeing miracles might excite the senses and get the adrenaline pumping. Having a strange vision might spur the imagination. An angelic appearance might make a dramatic impression. But these don't often penetrate deep within the heart, and they won't often drive us to repent of our sin. God's Word does just that.

Third, *the person who ignores the Word of God in life will be rejected by the God of the Word in eternity.* Don't want to wait until it's too late. The rich man waited—his opulent lifestyle too enjoyable to prompt him to seriously consider the true God. You don't want to find yourself in his position.

Are you a follower of Jesus Christ?

_____

If you said yes, what in your life reveals your status as a Christian? In what ways are you following Christ?

_____

_____

_____

_____

What reforms might you make as you seek to follow Christ ever more closely?

_____

_____

_____

_____

If you answered that you are _not_ a follower of Jesus, please turn to the back of this book, and read "How to Begin a Relationship with God."

Of all the _what ifs_ we can ask and all scenarios we can imagine, none is more certain than death . . . and none is more important to prepare for. When we stop and consider, we each have to admit that death could arrive on our doorsteps _tonight_. Are you in right relationship with God? Do you follow Jesus in faith and hope, embracing a life of love for God and others? Death has come near to all of us in one way or another—a beloved friend or family member dropping out of life just . . . like . . . that. Take the opportunity, right now, to make things right with the Lord.

When People Die . . . What Happens?

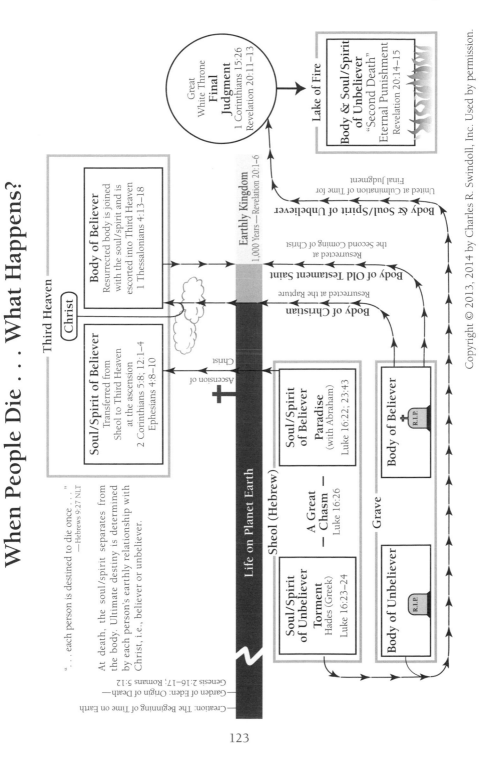

" . . . each person is destined to die once . . . "
—Hebrews 9:27 NLT

At death, the soul/spirit separates from the body. Ultimate destiny is determined by each person's earthly relationship with Christ, i.e., believer or unbeliever.

Creation: The Beginning of Time on Earth
Garden of Eden: Origin of Death—
Genesis 2:16–17; Romans 5:12

Life on Planet Earth

Third Heaven

Christ

Soul/Spirit of Believer
Transferred from
Sheol to Third Heaven
at the ascension
2 Corinthians 5:8; 12:1–4
Ephesians 4:8–10

Body of Believer
Resurrected body is joined
with the soul/spirit and is
escorted into Third Heaven
1 Thessalonians 4:13–18

Ascension of Christ

**Soul/Spirit
of Believer
Paradise**
(with Abraham)
Luke 16:22; 23:43

Body of Believer
R.I.P.

Sheol (Hebrew)

**A Great
— Chasm —**
Luke 16:26

**Soul/Spirit
of Unbeliever
Torment**
Hades (Greek)
Luke 16:23–24

Body of Unbeliever
R.I.P.

Grave

Earthly Kingdom
1,000 Years—Revelation 20:1–6

Body of Christian
Resurrected at the Rapture

Body of Old Testament Saint
Resurrected at
the Second Coming of Christ

Body & Soul/Spirit of Unbeliever
United at Culmination of Time for
Final Judgment

Great
White Throne
**Final
Judgment**
1 Corinthians 15:26
Revelation 20:11–13

Lake of Fire

**Body & Soul/Spirit
of Unbeliever
"Second Death"**
Eternal Punishment
Revelation 20:14–15

How to Begin a Relationship with God

Life is filled with questions. Many of these clamor for our attention even though the answers remain out of reach or are inconsequential. However, every person needs to take the opportunity to reflect on the most significant question for our lives today: *Whom do you follow?* Are you setting your path in the direction of the true God, or do you let others—or even yourself—decide on a different course of action?

What is the way to God, you ask? The Bible marks the path with four essential truths. Let's look at each marker in detail.

Our Spiritual Condition: Totally Depraved

The first truth is rather personal. One look in the mirror of Scripture, and our human condition becomes painfully clear:

> "There is none righteous, not even one;
> There is none who understands,
> There is none who seeks for God;
> All have turned aside, together they have become
> useless;
> There is none who does good,
> There is not even one." (Romans 3:10–12)

We are all sinners through and through—totally depraved. Now, that doesn't mean we've committed every atrocity known to human-kind. We're not as *bad* as we can be, just as *bad off* as we can be. Sin colors all our thoughts, motives, words, and actions.

If you've been around a while, you likely already believe it. Look around. Everything around us bears the smudge marks of our sin-ful nature. Despite our best efforts to create a perfect world, crime statistics continue to soar, divorce rates keep climbing, and families keep crumbling.

Something has gone terribly wrong in our society and in ourselves—something deadly. Contrary to how the world would repackage it, "me-first" living doesn't equal rugged individuality and freedom; it equals death. As Paul said in his letter to the Romans, "The wages of sin is death" (Romans 6:23)—our spiritual and physical death that comes from God's righteous judgment of our sin, along with all of the emotional and practical effects of this separation that we experience on a daily basis. This brings us to the second marker: God's character.

God's Character: Infinitely Holy

How can God judge us for a sinful state we were born into? Our total depravity is only half the answer. The other half is God's infinite holiness.

The fact that we know things are not as they should be points us to a standard of goodness beyond ourselves. Our sense of injustice in life on this side of eternity implies a perfect standard of justice beyond our reality. That standard and source is God Himself. And God's standard of holiness contrasts starkly with our sinful condition.

Scripture says that "God is Light, and in Him there is no darkness at all" (1 John 1:5). God is absolutely holy—which creates a problem for us. If He is so pure, how can we who are so impure relate to Him?

Perhaps we could try being better people, try to tilt the balance in favor of our good deeds, or seek out methods for self-improvement. Throughout history, people have attempted to live up to God's standard by keeping the Ten Commandments or living by their own code of ethics. Unfortunately, no one can come close to satisfying the demands of God's law. Romans 3:20 says, "By the works of the Law no flesh will be justified in His sight; for through the Law comes the knowledge of sin."

Our Need: A Substitute

So here we are, sinners by nature and sinners by choice, trying to pull ourselves up by our own bootstraps to attain a relationship with our holy Creator. But every time we try, we fall flat on our faces. We can't live a good enough life to make up for our sin, because God's standard isn't "good enough"—it's *perfection*. And we can't make amends for the offense our sin has created without dying for it.

Who can get us out of this mess?

If someone could live perfectly, honoring God's law, and would bear sin's death penalty for us—in our place—then we would be saved from our predicament. But is there such a person? Thankfully, yes!

Meet your substitute—*Jesus Christ*. He is the One who took death's place for you!

> [God] made [Jesus Christ] who knew no sin to be sin on our behalf, so that we might become the righteousness of God in Him. (2 Corinthians 5:21)

God's Provision: A Savior

God rescued us by sending His Son, Jesus, to die on the cross for our sins (1 John 4:9–10). Jesus was fully human and fully divine (John 1:1, 18), a truth that ensures His understanding of our weaknesses, His power to forgive, and His ability to bridge the gap between God and us (Romans 5:6–11). In short, we are "justified as a gift by His grace through the redemption which is in Christ Jesus" (Romans 3:24). Two words in this verse bear further explanation: *justified* and *redemption*.

Justification is God's act of mercy, in which He declares righteous the believing sinners while we are still in our sinning state. Justification doesn't mean that God *makes* us righteous, so that we never sin again, rather that He *declares* us righteous—much like a judge pardons a guilty criminal. Because Jesus took our sin upon Himself and suffered our judgment on the cross, God forgives our debt and proclaims us PARDONED.

Redemption is Christ's act of paying the complete price to release us from sin's bondage. God sent His Son to bear His wrath for all of our sins—past, present, and future (Romans 3:24–26; 2 Corinthians 5:21). In humble obedience, Christ willingly endured the shame of the cross for our sake (Mark 10:45; Romans 5:6–8; Philippians 2:8). Christ's death satisfied God's righteous demands. He no longer holds our sins against us, because His own Son paid the penalty for them. We are freed from the slave market of sin, never to be enslaved again!

Placing Your Faith in Christ

These four truths describe how God has provided a way to Himself through Jesus Christ. Because the price has been paid in full by God, we must respond to His free gift of eternal life in total faith and confidence in Him to save us. We must step forward into the relationship with God that He has prepared for us—not by doing good works or by being a good person, but by coming to Him just as we are and accepting His justification and redemption by faith.

> For by grace you have been saved through faith;
> and that not of yourselves, it is the gift of God;
> not as a result of works, so that no one may boast.
> (Ephesians 2:8–9)

We accept God's gift of salvation simply by placing our faith in Christ alone for the forgiveness of our sins. Would you like to enter a relationship with your Creator by trusting in Christ as your Savior? If so, here's a simple prayer you can use to express your faith:

Dear God,

I know that my sin has put a barrier between You and me.
Thank You for sending Your Son, Jesus, to die in my place.
I trust in Jesus alone to forgive my sins, and I accept His
gift of eternal life. I ask Jesus to be my personal Savior and
the Lord of my life. Thank You. In Jesus's name, amen.

If you've prayed this prayer or one like it and you wish to find out more about knowing God and His plan for you in the Bible, contact us at Insight for Living Ministries. Our contact information is on the following pages.

We Are Here for You

If you desire to find out more about knowing God and His plan for you in the Bible, contact us. Insight for Living Ministries provides staff pastors who are available for free written correspondence or phone consultation. These seminary-trained and seasoned counselors have years of experience and are well-qualified guides for your spiritual journey.

Please feel welcome to contact your regional office by using the information below:

United States

Insight for Living Ministries
Biblical Counseling Department
Post Office Box 5000
Frisco, Texas 75034-0055
USA
972-473-5097 (Monday through Friday,
8:00 a.m. – 5:00 p.m. central time)
www.insight.org/contactapastor

Canada

Insight for Living Canada
Biblical Counseling Department
PO Box 8 Stn A
Abbotsford BC V2T 6Z4
CANADA
1-800-663-7639
info@insightforliving.ca

Australia, New Zealand, and South Pacific

Insight for Living Australia
Pastoral Care
Post Office Box 443
Boronia, VIC 3155
AUSTRALIA
1300 467 444

United Kingdom and Europe

Insight for Living United Kingdom
Pastoral Care
PO Box 553
Dorking
RH4 9EU
UNITED KINGDOM
0800 787 9364
+44 1306 640156
pastoralcare@insightforliving.org.uk

Endnotes

Lesson Two

1. Karl Tate, "Hurricane Katrina History and Numbers," LiveScience, http://www.livescience.com/11235-hurricane-katrina-history-numbers.html (accessed January 2, 2014).

Lesson Three

1. Rowan Williams, *Dostoevsky: Language, Faith, and Fiction* (Waco, Tex.: Baylor University Press, 2008), 171.

Lesson Ten

1. Benedict of Nursia, *The Rule of St. Benedict in English*, ed. Timothy Fry (Vintage Spiritual Classics: Collegeville, Minn., 1981), 19.

Lesson Twelve

1. Wendell Berry, *Jayber Crow* (Berkley, Calif.: Counterpoint, 2000), 129.

Resources for Probing Further

We hope your time spent with the *What If . . . ? Bible Companion* has given you some answers to pressing questions that beset your way. All of us appreciate finding some firm ground to stand upon as we seek answers to the "what do we do" questions of life. While this book has certainly started the process of helping you become more like Christ, you might find yourself looking for other resources. We've listed several below. Of course, we cannot always endorse everything a writer or ministry says, so we encourage you to approach these and all other non-biblical resources with wisdom and discernment.

Bailey, Mark. *To Follow Him: The Seven Marks of a Disciple*. Portland: Multnomah Books, 1997.

Bonhoeffer, Dietrich. *The Cost of Discipleship*. New York: Touchstone, 1995.

Bridges, Jerry. *The Pursuit of Holiness*. Colorado Springs: NavPress, 2006.

Keller, Timothy. *Encounters with Jesus: Unexpected Answers to Life's Biggest Questions*. New York: Dutton, 2013.

Sanders, Oswald. *Spiritual Maturity: Principles of Spiritual Growth for Every Believer*. Chicago: Moody Publishers, 2007.

Swindoll, Charles R. *So You Want to Be Like Christ? Eight Essentials to Get You There*. Nashville: Thomas Nelson, 2005.

Yancey, Philip. *The Question that Never Goes Away*. Grand Rapids: Zondervan, 2014.

Ordering Information

If you would like to order additional copies of *What If . . . ? Bible Companion* or other Insight for Living Ministries resources, please contact the office that serves you.

United States

Insight for Living Ministries
Post Office Box 5000
Frisco, Texas 75034-0055
USA
1-800-772-8888
(Monday through Friday, 7:00 a.m. – 7:00 p.m. central time)
www.insight.org
www.insightworld.org

Canada

Insight for Living Canada
PO Box 8 Stn A
Abbotsford BC V2T 6Z4
CANADA
1-800-663-7639
www.insightforliving.ca

Australia, New Zealand, and South Pacific

Insight for Living Australia
Post Office Box 443
Boronia, VIC 3155
AUSTRALIA
1300 467 444
www.insight.asn.au

United Kingdom and Europe

Insight for Living United Kingdom
PO Box 553
Dorking
RH4 9EU
UNITED KINGDOM
0800 787 9364
+44 1306 640156
www.insightforliving.org.uk

Other International Locations

International constituents may contact the U.S. office through our Web site (www.insightworld.org), mail queries, or by calling +1-972-473-5136.